Robert Petkovšek,
Bojan Žalec (Eds.)

Truth and Compassion

Theology East – West
European Perspectives
Theologie Ost – West
Europäische Perspektiven

edited by

Prof. Dr. Janez Juhant
(University of Ljubljana)

and

Prof. Dr. Albert Franz
(University of Dresden)

Volume 20

LIT

TRUTH AND COMPASSION

Lessons from the Past and Premonitions of the Future

edited by

Robert Petkovšek and Bojan Žalec

LIT

Cover image: Alenka Doblekar, Photomontage

This book is printed on acid-free paper.

Bibliographic information published by the Deutsche Nationalbibliothek
The Deutsche Nationalbibliothek lists this publication in the Deutsche Nationalbibliografie; detailed bibliographic data are available on the Internet at http://dnb.d-nb.de.

ISBN 978-3-643-90773-8

A catalogue record for this book is available from the British Library

Klosbachstr. 107
CH-8032 Zürich
Tel. +41 (0) 44-251 75 05
E-Mail: zuerich@lit-verlag.ch http://www.lit-verlag.ch

Distribution:

In the UK: Global Book Marketing, e-mail: mo@centralbooks.com
In North America: International Specialized Book Services, e-mail: orders@isbs.com
In Germany: LIT Verlag Fresnostr. 2, D-48159 Münster
Tel. +49 (0) 2 51-620 32 22, Fax +49 (0) 2 51-922 60 99, e-mail: vertrieb@lit-verlag.de
In Austria: Medienlogistik Pichler-ÖBZ, e-mail: mlo@medien-logistik.at
e-books are available at www.litwebshop.de

Acknowledgments

We thank to all persons who have contributed to the appearing of the book. Our special thanks go to: the reviewers Professor Ciril Sorč and Assoc. Professor Michal Valčo; to Valerija Japelj for proofreading and corrections of the manuscript; to Vojko Strahovnik for help by editing; to Samo Grčman for the layout; and last but not least, to all the authors of the book.

This book was prepared and published with the support of Slovenian Research Agency (ARRS) and research programme P6-0269 (A) Ethical-religious grounds and perspectives of the society and the religious studies in context of education and violence.

Robert Petkovšek and Bojan Žalec, the editors

Ljubljana, September 2016

CONTENTS

INTRODUCTION

Why have we chosen the topic truth and compassion? In any case our starting point is the belief that the truth will set us free (Jn 8,32). Truth and compassion are doubtless connected. This is also the main point of two essays included in this collection and written by **Mateja Pevec Rozman** and **Erika Prijatelj**. We believe that, on one hand, without compassion we cannot reach the existentially important truths and that, on the other hand, the concealment of truth and lie often hinder or even make compassion impossible. The unhappy evidence for this truth is brought not only by the Slovenian not so distant history, but also by the contemporary events when we ask ourselves – meeting migrants and refugees – what is real truth about them and this – independently of whether we like it or not – influences our compassion for them. The latter problems sadly contribute to the actuality of the book.

This book consists of 17 essays written by 18 authors who cultivate different approaches since they come from different environments and scientific disciplines. Among them, there are representatives of theology, religious studies, philosophy, (intellectual) history, (social) psychology and psychotherapy, science of education, and legal science. They come from five different countries: Hungary, Poland, Russia, Romania, and Slovenia. So, the majority share personal experience of the non-democratic Communist regime. Regarding this fact it should not surprise us that some of them consider truth and compassion in the context of communism and communistic violence, but also of other totalitarian regimes.

Communism and totalitarianism

Jože Dežman deals with taboo of the communist violence and killings in Slovenia. This implied the concealing of the truth about their victims and making the compassion with them impossible. But, the truth survived and has been coming more and more to the light. **Tomaž Erzar** and **Katarina Kompan Erzar** are interested in the problem how to help the victims of the mentioned violence (in Slovenia). They stress the importance of the awareness of victims that they themselves have been forgiven. This makes them capable to get in touch with the goodness in them and around them, and to move from the position of a helpless victim to the position of a free and equal person being equal among the others. They stop being servants and become sons of the Father, all in need of forgiveness and compassion. **Stanko Gerjolj** investigates the nature and the dimensions of hell from the psychological aspect. Hell is the situation in which truth is misrepresented while people are not allowed to speak about the real truth. Such hell was "created" in the Communist regimes. The way to deconstruct hell is not hate towards its "creators", the perpetrators in it, and to those who were pushed in it, respectively. Quite to the contrary! Compassion is the way to breakthrough to experiential truth and this truth opens the way to actual truth. **Gábor Kovács,** by means of a concrete example of the communist believer György Lukács, throws the light upon the psychological aspect of such a believer. The communist ideology demanded from its believers a complete intellectual and moral conversion. Only in few months, Lukács went through such process: from the starting position that it is impossible to accept bolshevism because it wants to reach truth by the way of lie; to his final and life lasting account which accepts sin as a means for achieving the goals, and which forms the basis for immorality, irresponsibility, cruelty and criminality that are so characteristic for the communist movement and its intellectuals. Lukács was after the WW II marginalised but despite this fact, he remained a communist believer till his death. **Robert Petkovšek** utilizes the view of Alain Besançon on communism. He complements it with the findings of René Girard, Blaise Pascal, Aleksander Solzhenitsyn, and Carl von Clausewitz. In the focus of his essay are the topics of violence, lie and truth. He points to the role of institunalized lie in communism and concludes that communism was based on it. He compares Nazism with communism and establishes that the later is more stubborn than the first. He explains that the opposite of truth is not lie but violence. Following the way of truth in this sense is the way out of the circle of violence. To the group of essays that are more directly connected with totalitarianism, we may count also **Simon Malmenvall's** and **Vojko Strahovnik's** papers. The first critically presents the views of the Russian Orthodox theologian Georges Florovsky who claimed that the refusal of the Orthodox Christianity paved the way to the bolshevist revolution. Malmenvall partly agrees with Florovsky yet remains critical toward him stressing the fact that Florovsky did not take into account the situation in Russia integrally enough. Strahovnik's motivation for the dealing with his issue is the discussions (in Slovenia) whether we should leave the history to experts, whether we should allow the revision of historiography etc. He is interested in the importance of the historical truth for the integrity of community, and the significance of both for reconciliation. He defends a relatively holistic view on truth and finds out that the bearer of the truth value of the historical truth can only be some kind of integral narrative. In the second, ethical part of his essay he stresses that for the reaching of reconciliation, it is necessary to hear the stories of victims. The destruction, falsification or deformation of the history of a particular group of people is a crime against those people that undermines the integrity of their community. But, exactly this integrity is a necessary condition for the realization of the reconciliation processes at the communitarian level.

Tolerance, multiculturality and pluralism

Three essays deal with the problems of tolerance, multiculturality and pluralism. **Béla Mester** researches the need for a new concept of tolerance in the contemporary political context. Such tolerance is based on the recognitional attitude towards the tolerated. It takes into account also those things that are a matter of pride to him/her/them. A Russian social psychologist **Mark Kleyman**, who deals with the issues of multiculturality in the modern urban environments, in his paper refuses the position of the levelling multiculturalism, which takes all cultures as equal, as obviously false. Instead of it, he stresses – on the basis of solidary personalism, which he connects with the thought of Lev Tolstoy and Albert Schweitzer – the importance of defending of human dignity that can serve as a foundation for the cultivation of the right tolerance. **Anton Jamnik** stresses the need for the convergence of our views despite his recognition of diversity and plurality. We need a minimal ethical cultural common denominator, "world ethos", which is a precondition for mutual dialogue and makes possible that we coexist in peace and shape our societies and world together. As Kleyman, he stresses the importance of respect for human dignity and proposes some principles of such a minimal common ethos, which should be respected by all. From this general starting point he develops his ideas about ethical issues of research on human beings and medical care. His views are strongly based on the ethical documents of the relevant reputable institutions.

Art of life and the meaning of faith and transcendence

The third complex consists of the essays that are not primarily societally oriented but belong more to the areas of art of life, philosophical and theological anthropology, transcendental issues and metaphysics. **Roman Globokar** enlightens the topic of a life decision. He leans upon the theory of Klaus Demmer (1931–2014), one of the leading Catholic moral theologians after Vatican II. From this point of view, Globokar considers marriage and celibacy and finds out that the level of indissolubility is the same by both. **Stanislav Slatinek** deals with the abuse of truth in marriage and its fatal consequences in the light of the judgements of the Court of the Roman Rota (1993–2003).

Despite common stressing of the importance of truth and compassion by the authors of the book, some of them point out also to the dangers hidden in inappropriate striving for both. One of them is **Marcin Godawa** from Krakow. He warns against the trap of compassion when we only insist by some problem without solving it actively. Thus, for example, today compassion is politically correct but it does not include a real intention to find a solution for those to whom our compassion is directed. This trap is the consequence of detaching of empathy from the integral truth about man. In this context, Godawa deals with God's grace. He presents the liberating force of Grace. Grace is a gift of the Spirit. Godawa reminds us of the thought of St. Pope John Paul II that Grace speaks to an individual person. He stresses the gentleness of the act of the Spirit who comes with the gentleness of the Truth, and as a protector. The Spirit comes with the truth and can help man, He can move him/her and show him/her the way out from any situation. The main topic of the essay of **Marcel Măcelaru** is human flourishing. His thesis is that it is possible only on the basis of a proper relationship of man with God. This is the common point of his position with **Bojan Žalec's** account. Žalec presents Charles Bellinger's interpretation of the origins of human violence and pathology according to which they both originate in the disturbances at the three dimensions of human existence: man-God, development of the human self, and the social dimension (man : man). Bellinger's thought is strongly influenced by Kierkegaard. The main staring point of both is that man is called by God to become a unique image of God. Man's refusal of this call is the basic origin of his/her violence and pathology, and the ways to ignore it, to hide from it, to silence it, to "destroy" it etc. represent the fundamental forms of them. Thus man's refusal of the truth – at this fundamental level – about who she/he is and who should she/he become results in violence and in lack of compassion (as its condition).

Robert Petkovšek and Bojan Žalec, the editors

RENUNCIATION OF LIE – WAY OUT OF VIOLENCE

Robert Petkovšek, Ljubljana

Violence in an anthropological framework

René Girard published a work titled *Achever Clausewitz* (*Battling to the End*) in 2007 as a commentary to the unfinished and posthumously published work *Vom Kriege* (1832) by the Prussian General, military reformer and theoretician Carl von Clausewitz (1780–1831). This work shows, according to Girard, that Clausewitz not only grasps the reality of human nature, which is inherently contrary, but also correctly prophesies the future of western society. Girard is convinced this is "perhaps one of the greatest books on war ever published" (Girard 2007, 13) and that without this work it would be impossible "to understand the drama of modern world" (32).

Girard finds in Clausewitz an inspiration and confirmation of his mimetic theory, which considers mimetic desire, i.e., the desire to imitate and compare, the driving force of human culture. This desire is inherently contrary: at once creative and destructive, unifying and sundering. The driving force of human nature, according to Clausewitz, is *polemos,* duel, desire to dominate, which manifests itself at all levels of human life, from daily conflicts among relatives and neighbors to wars in the broadest sense. Clausewitz understands well that reciprocity is the essential and fundamental characteristic of every relationship, which means that every gesture encourages a counter-gesture, every act its counter-act. As a result, parties in a relationship become alike. This similarity is at the origin of comparison, measuring of strength, tendency to duel and dominate.

This brings us to the central thesis of Clausewitz, that every duel, even the smallest, has an intrinsic tendency toward absolute domination, i.e., tendency to absolute escalation of violence to extremes; this intuition is called "apocalyptic formula" by Girard (2007, 15), and reveals the truth that violence is an absolute notion: any violence hides a "tendency to escalation to extremes." Man and his culture are the result of human hyper-mimetic desire, which differentiates humans from other living beings. Human desire is hyper-mimetic in essence, i.e., desire and imitation cannot be stopped: the stronger the obstacle the stronger the desire. Hence, human desire is not only creative but also destructive and is at the origin of violence that is capable of going to extremes, beyond any limits.

Humanity has from the very beginning lived with the intuition that it can be destroyed by the hyper-mimetic desire, which leads to the 'duel,' argues Clausewitz. Humanity has found an answer to this problem in institutions, which are solid and set forms of collective behavior, stresses Girard. The first and founding institution was the 'sacrifice of the scapegoat,' which was intended to stop the escalation of hyper-mimetic desire to extreme and inhumane forms of violence that would transform man into a *monstrum* (diabolic violence) or even destroy humanity (apocalyptic violence). Other religious (rituals and myths) and social institutions (laws and government) constitute the superstructure upon the first and original institution of the scapegoat; their founding purpose is just as much to limit the hyper-mimetic desire so as to keep it from developing into extreme forms of violence, toward which it tends in its essence. The function of the original 'institution of the scapegoat' is to channel and polarize the violence that spreads infectiously through the community onto one single powerless and innocent victim; it is thus the *transformation* of uncontrolled violence ("struggle of all against all") into controlled violence ("struggle of all against one"). The essence of the scapegoat mechanism is therefore polarization of violence, i.e., the channeling of uncontrolled universal violence onto one single powerless and innocent victim in order to return stability to the community.

Girard recognizes that Clausewitz, a contemporary of Napoleon, was a prophet who foresaw the breakdown of institutions, beginning with Napoleon. Disintegration of institutions also means "deculturalization" and implies an ever diminishing capacity of man to control hyper-mimetic desire with its tendency toward escalation to extremes. Considered by Girard a prophet of apocalypse, Clausewitz was right indeed; his apocalyptic insights came close to fulfillment a century later.

It is therefore clear to both Clausewitz and Girard that history is not self-evident directional progress but rather the resultant of counteracting forces that does not bring only progress but also the danger of self-destruction. Human history is thus not only a history of progress but also a history of violence, which in our modern post-Napoleonic civilization got the chance to erupt in extreme, inhuman, demonic and apocalyptic forms.

Violence in a metaphysical framework

We have just addressed the question of violence at its anthropological level. Violence, from this perspective, has its origin in the contrary human nature: history is the resultant of the duel, according to Clausewitz, and of the human hyper-mimetic desire, according to Girard. It is significant that Girard chooses to begin his commentary to Clausewitz's work with a thought from the 12th *Provincial Letter* by Blaise Pascal and thus moves the discourse from the anthropological to the metaphysical level. Pascal emphasizes in the passage that it is impossible to understand violence without its fundamental attribute, its relation to the truth.

"It is a strange and tedious war when violence attempts to vanquish truth. All the efforts of violence cannot weaken truth, and only serve to give it fresh vigor. All the lights of truth cannot arrest violence, and only serve to exasperate it. When force meets force, the weaker must succumb to the stronger; when argument is opposed to argument, the solid and the convincing triumphs over the empty and the false; but violence and verity can make no impression on each other. Let none suppose, however, that the two are, therefore, equal to each other; for there is this vast difference between them, that violence has only a certain course to run, limited by the appointment of Heaven, which overrules its effects to the glory of the truth which it assails; whereas verity endures forever and eventually triumphs over its enemies, being eternal and almighty as God himself." (Pascal 1963, 429; in: Girard 2007, 7) [this quotation translated by Thomas M'Crie]

How are violence and truth related, according to Pascal? Their relationship is certainly not univocal, causal, intentional or dialectic: violence attempts to weaken truth but on the contrary ends up strengthening it; truth tries to stop violence but on the contrary ends up provoking it. Violence would therefore want to influence truth and truth influence violence; however, just the opposite is happening, i.e., "violence and truth have no effect on each other." Neither violence nor truth succeeds in its purpose, as the results of their actions are unexpected and contrary to the intended. As for violence, greater violence triumphs over the lesser, and as for truth, weaker truth fades next to stronger truth. There is no real reciprocity or proportionality between violence and truth. Relationship between the two is not logical. The aim of violence is to *suppress* truth, whereas it ultimately elevates truth. The aim of truth is to stop violence, whereas it ultimately provokes violence. Their action thus brings paradoxically unexpected results. Their influence is not as planned, which is why Pascal concludes that they "have no effect on each other."

Nevertheless, violence and truth are not neutral toward each other. On the contrary, as Pascal explains, there is "a strange and tedious war" between the two; each wants to vanquish the other. Violence and truth are therefore in opposition. Moreover, they are disproportional and incompatible phenomena, which is why it is impossible to gauge them with the same measure. This is the essence of what Pascal has written above. He sees a "vast difference" between the two, which is as follows, "violence has only a certain course to run, limited by the appointment of Heaven, which overrules its effects to the glory of the truth which it assails; whereas verity endures forever and eventually triumphs over its enemies, being eternal and almighty as God himself." One thus cannot apply the same measure to violence and truth, as they are not at the same level. Pascal places truth at the level of God, whereas violence is not at the level of God and truth. Nevertheless, violence struggles against truth.

Truth is eternal and strong, as God Himself. Violence sees in truth its opponent and thus attacks it. Therefore, violence is an opponent, un-truth and lie in relation to truth. In addition, violence is not eternal but temporal. What is then the function of violence?

Pascal has thus struck at the essence of man. Man is not only a biological and cultural being but also a metaphysical being, and as such he is not univocal but inherently unpredictable, an unknown to himself. Pascal keeps searching for the right term to express this unknown; to him, man is at once "the pride and refuse of the universe."

"What a chimera, then, is man! What a novelty! What a monster, what a chaos, what a contradiction, what a prodigy! Judge of all things, imbecile worm of the earth; depositary of truth, a sink of uncertainty and error; the pride and refuse of the universe! … Know then, proud man, what a paradox you are to yourself. Humble yourself, weak reason; be silent, foolish nature; learn that man infinitely transcends man." (Pascal 2003, § 434)

Girard shows by citing Pascal at the beginning of his commentary to Clausewitz that hyper-mimetic desire is not the ultimate answer to the mystery of violence but that the answer can be found in its metaphysical background constituted by the relationship of man to truth and God. Girard would not deny any of the terms Pascal uses to describe man. Mimetic theory sees and recognizes at once the greatness and smallness of man; it understands human existence is a paradox.

Pascal defines man a metaphysical paradox. Paradox is the very category that helps understand man in his angelic or demonic metamorphosis and enables us to think about the relational coexistence of violence and truth. How should we understand paradox? Friedrich Dürenmatt considers Oedipus an example of paradoxical existence, "People who make deliberate progress want to accomplish a certain goal, which is why they are most afflicted by coincidence, if they accomplish just the opposite of their goal because of it: what they fear the most … like Oedipus … Such a story is not contrary to meaning. It is a paradox." (Dürrenmatt 1980, Anhang 21) Kierkegaard gave the category of paradox a central role, for it is possible to consider the contradictions of life in the light of paradox, as was done by the Gospels, which is why paradox is "higher than any system" (Kierkegaard 1909–, Pap. II, A 439). Therein lies the special capacity of the Christian spirit, which is distinct from philosophy, "The idea of philosophy is mediation; the idea of Christianity is paradox." (Pap. III, A 108) Therefore, the essence of paradox is to tolerate the coexistence of two absolutely different qualities, temporality and eternity, for example, or immanence and transcendence. Kierkegaard concludes by stating paradox is a "category, an ontological determination that expresses the relationship between existing spirit and truth" (Pap. VIII/1, A 11). 'Truth of spirit' is thus paradoxical. Hence, Kierkegaard says effectively the same as Pascal: man is capable of being what he is not; he can not only be his dialectic opposite but also go beyond, go so far as to become unrecognizable to himself. This is what Sophocles wanted to express in the character of Oedipus or Pascal in terms such as 'chimera' and 'monster.'

The essence of the relationship between truth and violence is thus concealed in human existence and its paradoxical nature. The capacity to know the truth doubtlessly makes human human. However, the truth about truth is undefinable. What does truth ultimately lead us to? It leads us to knowledge that can be empirically concrete, theoretically formal, philosophically holistic and original, vitally wise and finally religiously redemptive. Truth is a multilevel and multilayer notion. Most generally accepted definition of truth is its being an agreement between thought and object of thought. However, truths of life are not only agreements between reason and its object but also even deeper agreements between the way of life and meaning of life. The same is true of religious truths; religious truths that are not lived by the faithful are empty and void of meaning. John Caputo states the word *God* is not a theoretical notion but a call to conversion, which is why he thinks the appropriate translation of the word is not semantic but existential. Therefore, faith is originally expressed not by words but by the way of life. Truth thus enlightens man and leads him on the way through reality and life to the fullness of being, which is salvation, according to religious belief. Religions stress one cannot fathom the ultimate truth about oneself in God, i.e., about one's own super-humanity. This remains a mystery and an 'object' of mystic experience. One can say the same about truth, which Pascal has placed beside God. Relationship between man and his ultimate truth transcends rational categories and is thus paradoxical, as has been stressed by mystics.

Violence at a historical level

Let us now consider the historical level. Man is a historical being. Concrete historical circumstances are the venue of human exercise of free will and manifest all of the paradoxicalness of human existence. Truth does not protect man in advance from becoming un-human. Truth reveals and liberates; therein lies its essence: by liberating man for doing more good and thus more fully fulfill himself, it also liberates him for evil. In this sense, truth provokes and allows violence. Truth releases man and thus exposes him also to the possibility of escalation of violence to extremes, to the demonic and apocalyptic violence witnessed in the 20th century. Let us mention the testimonies given by Primo Levi and Emmanuel Lévinas.

In his book titled *L'humanité perdue: essai sur le XXe siècle* (1996, 7–11) Alain Finkielkraut tries to find a term for the inhumanity that reached its abyss in the 20th century. He finds a description of this inhumanity in the work *If This Is a Man: Survival in Auschwitz* (1947) by the Jewish Italian chemist and author Primo Levi who survived the holocaust. Levi describes his interrogation in Auschwitz by Doktor Pannwitz, who was selecting workers among prisoners for his engineering team, as follows: "His gaze was not that of a man toward another man; if one could describe the nature of this gaze, exchanged as if across aquarium glass between two beings, each of which belonged to another world, one would at once explain the essence of the great folly of the Third Reich." (Levi 1987, 138) This attitude that defies recognition of humanity and solidarity is summed up by Finkielkraut in the term 'un-human.' An 'un-human' has thus stepped out of a human. Finkielkraut finds that Emmanuel Lévinas has had similar experience and described his life in the camp as follows: "The other passers-by who were called 'free' and who gave us work and orders were stripping us of human skin. Only the poor internal sighs were reminding us of our rational essence. But we ourselves were no longer in the world." One day a dog appeared among the prisoners of the camp; he was called Bobby by the prisoners dreaming about America. He greeted them at the roll call in the morning or upon their returning from work, barking and wagging his tail. "It was unarguably clear to him: we were people." A few weeks later the guards chased him away, and thus was expelled – concludes Lévinas – "the last Kantian of Nazi Germany as well" (Lévinas 1976, 201; 202).

The two accounts speak of the un-human every man harbors within himself and cannot stop. Man has thus been revealed as a *monstrum*, the demonic form that exceeds human capabilities and framework. There is nothing human in demonic forms of evil. Therefore, if truth provokes violence, how is it possible then for truth to provoke and enable violence to assume such extreme, inhuman, demonic forms?

Many have tried to address the problem of the conditions that allowed extreme forms of violence and that made demonic and apocalyptic violence possible. Aleksandr Solzhenitsyn has analyzed the phenomenon of violence within the Soviet communist system and concisely summarized his findings in an appeal to the Soviet people titled *Live Not By Lies!* on February 12, 1974, a few days before his expulsion from the Soviet Union. He has elucidated the inner link between lie and violence. He is convinced that violence spreads by lie and is maintained by lie. A culture founded on lie leads to spiritual death, which he says will "consume us both and our children." In such a situation, which he describes as *hopelessly dehumanized*, man is prepared to betray everything — principles, soul, efforts of ancestors and opportunities for posterity — only for a small ration of food and to not perturb his fragile existence. Such a man is indifferent to pride, fidelity and excitement. He fears nothing, not even nuclear war nor World War III, but he fears acts of civilian courage, being left behind the herd, being lonely, without bread or without gas for heating. Ideological indoctrination is thus saturated with the idea of comfortable life. This is the first aspect of the lie into which Soviet society was sinking. The second aspect, points out Solzhenitsyn, is the conviction of the "young and presumptuous people who thought they would make our country just and happy through terror, bloody rebellion and civil war." Solzhenitsyn replies to these "fathers of education," "No, thanks!" He is convinced that "infamous methods breed infamous results." Solzhenitsyn thus describes the situation into which the Soviet people were pushed by communist ideology. What enabled and maintained such a situation? "Nothing," he says, "will ever happen as long as we daily acknowledge, extol, and strengthen—and do not sever ourselves from the most perceptible of its aspects: Lies." He thus shows the internal link between violence and lie; he considers lie bearer of violence, by which violence maintains and regenerates itself. Violence is violent; when it invades peaceful life, it beams self-confidence as if carrying a banner, "I am violence. Run away, make way for me—I will crush you!" However, violence soon "grows old" and loses self-confidence; in order to preserve its honor, it seeks allies in lie, untruth and falsehood. From then on violence "lays its ponderous paw not every day and not on every shoulder. It demands from us only obedience to lies and daily participation in lies—all loyalty lies in that."

Sovietologist Alain Besançon goes even further in his analysis of the link between violence and lie; in his work *A Century of Horrors* (French *Le malheur du siècle*) he deals with destructive physical, moral and political consequences of Nazism and Communism. His conclusion is clear: destructive power of Communism was deeper and more fateful than that of Nazism. Curiously, the two totalitarian systems turned traditional morality upside down. Besançon calls traditional morality "natural and common morality," the core of which consists of basic commandments or prohibitions, such as "Do not kill!" or "Do not steal!" In spite of differences, traditional cultures were unified in terms of basic norms. He understands "natural or common morality" as "morality that is talked about by ancient Greek and Roman sages, as well as Chinese, Indian and African sages" (2014, 52); through millennia it has developed a specific idea about reality. However, in contrast to this reality, both totalitarianisms – Nazism and Communism – wanted to create a new reality, which Besançon characterizes as 'pseudo-reality' (59). The term 'pseudo-reality' means false reality, i.e., reality which opposes truth and is thus violent. Lie is thus more or less effective. Every lie is not equally strong and equally far-reaching. By comparing Nazism and Communism Besançon tries to address the question of how lie works, and what makes lie stronger in creating pseudo-reality. He has studied it from many perspectives: goals and justification of goals, means to accomplishment of goals; liturgical character of the language of both totalitarianisms; their ethics and demonic character.

Both totalitarianisms use the word 'good' to describe their *goals*, which begs the question of how they understand the word. The answer to the question of violence is therefore concealed in the understanding and interpretation of the word 'good.' Their intention is to change man and create a new society that will be simply *good.* Nazism is convinced that our society is not good, since it is based on Christianity, which has upturned the order of races; a good society is based on natural order. Nazism sets out to cleanse humanity of the Christian spirit. "If we do not find again this moral connection, the most profound and the best, since it is most natural, we will not be capable at this level to vanquish Christianity and establish this German Reich that will be a blessing for the entire earth. It has been the task of the fair race for millennia to rule the earth and to ever bring it happiness and civilization" (Himmler, 9. 6. 1942, in: Besançon 2014, 42). Furthermore, Christianity is a "plague, the worst disease that has stricken us in all of our history" (42). It has given rise to other disasters: democracy, bolshevism, rule of gold, Jews. Nazism thus intends to reestablish the natural order of races; it understands its mission as cleansing, the goal of which is to exterminate troublesome insects, 'lice.' This shall be the 'final solution': "Destruction of lice does not arise from a concept of the world. It is a question of hygiene. [...] Soon we shall no longer have lice." This is about "a racial, primitive, natural and original struggle" (Himmler, 24. 4. and 1. 12. 1943, in: Besançon 2014, 43). Communism emphasizes even more that its goal is the creation of a new man with new morality, which shall replace the old capitalistic morality, which is full of injustice and oppression. The path to the new man and new morality is revolution, which makes use of any means, even demonic, in order to accomplish its goals. Both systems introduce their goals with the word 'good.' The former understands the word to mean a return to natural order and the latter to mean a revolutionary creation of a new society. Besançon formulates such understanding of the word 'good' in a phrase he uses for the title of one of his works, *Falsification of the Good* (French *Falsification du Bien*), where he shows how two of the greatest minds of the 20th century, Vladimir Solovyov and George Orwell, understood the falsification of the good as the fundamental problem of Communism.

Besançon reckons that Nazi Germany was morally polarized with regard to the means used to accomplish its goals. Nazism did not succeed in destroying all of the tradition. The letters by Heinrich Himmler (2014) show this founder and head of the Nazi concentration camps was an exemplary and sensitive family father. Besançon finds that "many grand executioners were indeed gentle family fathers and sentimental spouses" while they demanded of their troops to carry out their most cruel assignments calmly, without 'egoistic' motives (Besançon 2014, 44–45). Delinquencies such as drunkenness, rape, theft and sadism were punished. It is therefore possible to find 'remnants of a legal system' in Nazism. Even in the officer corps, it was possible to find men who tried to preserve their honor. The movie titled *Schindler's List* shows businessmen who were hiring Jewish workers in order to save them. There were from the outset no such islands of legal safety in the Soviet Union, finds Besançon. On the other hand, the physical elimination of the Jewish people in Germany was a 'publicly known secret.' Nazi Germany had a double face: the close-knit circle of executioners was acting demonically to the point nobody could believe, not even the Jews standing in front of the gas chambers; outside of this circle there were islands of legal safety and remnants of traditional morality that Nazism was unable to subdue and destroy (45–49). Communism acted more holistically and profoundly. It understood its mission as a historical necessity that is revolutionary and dramatic. Stalin kept repeating, "It makes no sense to cry for spilled milk ... there are no roses without thorns ... the end sanctifies the means" (50). The declaration of Bakunin reflects the same uncompromising spirit, "The spirit of destruction is the same as the spirit of creation." (51) There can be nothing new without the uncompromising destruction of the old. Communism, that is, a new society founded on the example of the primitive human commune, is a goal that is absolutely good. The time between the primeval human community and communism is absolutely evil; there is nothing good in it. History is a struggle between the good and evil, which is why all means are allowed to achieve the good that is communism. Therefore, theft, lies, false testimony, mass killings, lawlessness, treason of the closest, all are justified by the goal that is wrapped in the highest human ideals. This outlook harbors a gnostic belief in absolute opposition of two origins, the origin of good and that of evil. In order to achieve the good we need to uncompromisingly root out the bad.

Besançon argues that *liturgical language*, which has the power to present an untrue and false image of reality, plays a special role in the construction of pseudo-reality. Nazism and communism have each created a liturgical language that is not intended to serve dialog, expression, criticality or search of truth, but is intended to mislead. They used its power and charm to draw the biggest intellectuals and artists of their time to serve their ideology. Nazism, for example, drew Martin Heidegger and Carl Schmitt, communism Bertolt Brecht, Pablo Picasso, Louis Aragon and others. Moreover, Besançon points out, one cannot explain the crimes committed in the name of these two ideologies only by the perpetrators of these acts but primarily by the ideological delusion that fascinated the perpetrators. The acts Eichmann "was accused of were not in proportion to the narrow conscience of this trite being" (49), finds Besançon. The two liturgical languages have drawn their power from having distorted the meaning of fundamental concepts of values. They have used terms of traditional morality such as justice, equality or freedom and assigned them completely different and distorted meaning. Communism has carried out this mechanism of ideological deception through distortion of meaning of traditional notions to the extreme. Such communist radicalness is most prominently displayed in the distortion of the old and universally accepted idea of the good, whereby whatever traditional morality considers good communism considers bad and whatever traditional morality considers bad communism considers good. Communism has carried out this distortion with utmost finesse, so that the twisted meaning remains hidden even to its adherents. Communist ideologues were clearly aware of the changes in the meaning of ideas, as is evident from the title of a work by Trotsky, *Their Morals and Ours*. Trotsky stresses that 'their' (i.e., traditional) morality is not 'ours' (i.e., communist). Old words thus stand for completely new ideas and notions (51). Philanthropic terms borrowed from traditional morality thus drew people with the highest moral ideals who did not suspect they were unwittingly accepting a morality that had nothing in common with the traditional one. This is perhaps the root cause of the collective amnesia of communist crimes, suggests Besançon (56). Communism has couched itself in terms of the purest common moral ideals, which Nazism has not even tried. This is likely the reason why the common conscience cannot forget and forgive the crimes of Nazism, whereas it benevolently and understandingly commits the crimes of communism to oblivion and does not condemn them. This is also the fundamental difference between Nazism and communism. Nazism was more radical and thorough than communism in the cruelty of crimes, whereas communism has developed to the extreme the capacity to distort and delude, which is shown most clearly in its distortion and falsification of the notion of 'good.' Nazism too has tried to present its crimes as something good but failed; communism, however, enthralls its adherents and many others even today, after the collapse of its strongholds, in the belief that its violence was necessary, good and justified. Communism is thus more dangerous than Nazism (56). Even the torture victims in Soviet camps have not called their torturers by the true name 'communists' but have used the term 'fascists', deliberately chosen in order to keep the word 'communism' unblemished.

Besançon uses the term 'pedagogy of lies' to denote the mechanism of distortion of meaning of the words that stand for the highest human ideals such that they conceal violence and crime. 'Pedagogy of lies' has enabled the genesis of a new (un)culture. The first step is to recruit new adherents. "In the beginning a significant part of the population receives pedagogy of lies in good faith. It accepts the new morality with its old moral legacy. It loves the leaders who are promising happiness and believes it is happy. It thinks it lives in a just world" (60). The second step is the creation of a mechanism for maintenance and dissemination of lies. It is necessary to clearly identify, hate and denounce the enemies of socialism; it is necessary to agree to robbery, murder and collaboration in crimes. The system increasingly closes in on itself by creating disinformation, false proofs and ignorance. Rational and moral guidelines are increasingly being lost. The difference between communism and the common moral ideals is being erased; responsibility for failures and abuses is being shifted to an external enemy. People who are blinded by the communist ideology gradually fail to recognize a crime as a crime and correctly call it by its true term. A specific spirit emerges, first at a hidden and subconscious level and then increasingly openly and consciously, which changes the self-image the people used to have. Cowardice, vileness and dejection begin to set in and spread. Wives begin to hate their husbands and children their parents, while they feel they are very much alike. This is followed by increasing irresponsibility, apathy, feeling of senselessness, reticence, sentimentality, self-pity; all of these merge into two basic feelings, hopelessness and disgust, as shown by the literature of this milieu. The entire social system has become an extended system of mutual control and denunciation. There were a few dissidents who stood in opposition, such as individual families, individual university departments (e.g., departments of classical philology), parts of the Church and some youth groups; Soviet camps were also places of intellectual freedom.

Ultimately, this begs the question of *ethics* in the two totalitarian systems. Nazi ideology was naturalistic; it was based on the idea of the superhuman and the will for power, on nihilism and irrationalism. Its frame of mind was esthetics, which is why it did not find advocates from the point of ethics. Its inhuman distortion was obvious, which is why it could not rise to the universal level. In contrast, communism used universal ethical framework; it spoke of virtue and moral imperative. Raymond Aron stresses that "the Soviet regime arose from a revolutionary will inspired by humanitarian ideals" and that its "goal was to create the most humane regime ever known in history, the first regime where all the people could have access to humanity, where social classes would disappear, where the homogeneity of society would allow mutual respect among citizens. However, this movement that tended toward an absolute goal would not hesitate to use any means, because its doctrine held that only violence could create that absolutely good society and that the proletariat was waging a merciless war against capitalism. This combination of a lofty goal and merciless technique gave rise to different stages of the Soviet regime." (Aron 1965, 302) Furthermore, "I would argue from the outset that regardless of the similarity between the two phenomena there is an essential difference. The difference is essential because of the ideas that inspire them. In one case, one ends up in a labor camp and in the other in a gas chamber. In one case, there is the willingness to build a new regime and perhaps a new man, regardless of the means. In the other case there is literally a demonic will to destroy a pseudo-race." (302) It is impossible to deny that communism was motivated by ethical goals, which were to create a better man and a better society, but communism pursued these goals extremely unethically. The conviction that it is possible to build love on hatred, brotherhood on enmity, and good on evil is the fundamental contradiction of communism. The good that is achieved through evil is not really good but only apparently good. This is how communist morality diverged from traditional common morality, which clearly distinguished good from evil, and thus unleashed the extreme monstrous violence that considered evil good and good evil. The evil that appeared good became uncontrollable; it outgrew human capacities and limits and thus became demonized.

Goals, means, liturgical language and demonic ethics lead to *pseudo-reality*, which is contrary to humanity and humanness (59). The pseudo-reality created by Nazism is impossible to express in words and notions; imagination finds it revolting and memory does not wish to retain it. It is outside of the human; it is demonic. Germany awoke after the war as if from a slumber (40). It became aware of the falsity and untruthfulness of the Nazi project; it admitted its own error and delusion. Much as the German gave in to this delusion at one time, he was awakening from it twenty years later. His understanding of reality was in this case a reversible process, capable of returning to the normal feel for reality. It was different with the fall of communism, which had imposed itself through promises of a humane society with equality and justice for all and based on the scientific view of the world. Communism progressively distanced itself from its initial promises. Lenin was convinced that the 'ultimate time' would appear immediately after the revolution had abolished capitalism once and for all. Since this did not come to pass, the regime began to substitute lies for the promises. Lies escalated as the discrepancy between the facts and words increased. Besançon discerns four stages in the development of communism (59–62). First, the Party is the center of all activity; the Party is completely under influence of a utopian ideology, the goal of which is to destroy the 'enemy of the class.' In the name of this ideology, communist systems in the beginning killed on the order of 10 % of the population (Russia, Korea, China, Poland and others). Second, the unfulfilled utopia is replaced by the desire for the preservation of power; the Party retains its power through total control of the population, spreading of fear, denunciation and spying. Third, the Party no longer believes in ideology; it creates its own discourse that it knows is false but is the only permitted discourse. This discourse is now the sign of power of the Party and ensures benefits and privileges; the population no longer compares Party members to "wolves" but to "pigs" (G. Orwell). Fourth, the Party ultimately closes down the state borders in order to hide its failures. The state becomes an extensive school of reeducation, making it impossible for the people to know the past and the present by creating a corps of false journalists and historians, false literature and arts, by making up statistics and creating a new language with liturgical value that gives words new meaning that is different from the one commonly accepted. Besançon concludes, "Construction of this immense decor employs millions of people;" its purpose is "to prove that socialism is not only possible but already under construction" (59–60). The aim of this decor is the 'pedagogy of lies;' its consequences are "psychological and mental damage," states Besançon (37). This is also the reason for the persistence of the characteristic fascination with communism in post-communist countries.

Conclusion

We have addressed the question of violence at three levels, anthropological, metaphysical and historical. Violence is a constitutive part of human history from the very beginning and is inseparably linked to anthropological structure. In the 20th century, it breached the bounds of anthropological structure and found expression in un-human demonic forms. Modern globalized society is ultimately threatened by violence of apocalyptic dimensions, with consequent self-destruction of humanity. Violence in the smallest form already harbors seeds of violence of demonic and apocalyptic proportions. Violence characteristically knows no bounds and tends to extremes that exceed anthropological limits; at this point one needs to look for reasons at the metaphysical level. Historical context gives importance to institutions, the original role of which is to restrain violence and its tendencies to extremes. Clausewitz has already noted that institutions within western society have been getting weaker and disintegrating, which has made eruption of extreme forms of violence possible; his prediction has come to pass in the demonic forms of Nazism and communism. These forms reveal uncontrollability of violence and its metaphysical origins.

Pascal has dealt with the metaphysics of violence; he has linked violence to the question of truth, which is "eternal, like God" and thus has divine attributes. Pascal argues that truth is invincible and everlasting, whereas violence is passing and vincible. His optimistic vision of victorious truth does not, however, deprive violence of the weight it has shown historically. Nazism and communism indicate there is 'surplus of evil', i.e., the kind of evil that surpasses the capacities of man and is thus un-human and demonic. "Who has the power in a pure Nazi or communist regime?" Besançon replies, "This simple question, which apparently was easier to answer than a similar question regarding any other regime, since the possessor of all powers was visible everywhere, and even obsessively visible — the Führer, the Secretary General, the Party —, constituted a profound enigma for those who were capable of philosophical reflection: Jünger, Platonov, Orwell, Miłosz, Zinovjev … They let it be heard what had been proclaimed by religious souls, Mandelstam, Ahmatova, Bulgakov, Rauschning, Herbert, Solzhenitsyn: It is the devil! It was him who communicated to his subjects his un-human impersonality. Dostoyevski and Vladimir Solovyov had this intuition in advance. It would be as if we had not listened faithfully to all these testimonies if we failed to mention this character." (2014, 86) Violence is thus not only a consequence of human weakness, which renders man incapable of humanizing his life; violence has its own bearer, its own subject, which stands in opposition to man. Many thinkers adopted a name for it, the 'devil.'

The original opponent of truth is not lie or un-truth but violence, according to Pascal, which leads one to conclude that truth is more than just a formal accordance between reason and thing. Truth that is opposed by violence is the profound good, closeness, nonviolence, peace, love, benevolence, compassion, life. This is truth in its most profound essence, which religions call by a personal name God and the Gospel calls Jesus Christ. Violence only confirms it: violence presents itself as something good and as truth itself, but it manifests itself falsely as truth and finds refuge in lies. Truth is thus the bearer of good to the extent that it is not violent even to violence or that it does not prevent neither violence nor lie.

Lie and violence are profoundly tied and intertwined. Besançon writes that communism has highly perfected the power of lie, which it has used to hide its crimes. This is borne out by the statement made by an editor of the French socialist paper *L'humanité* in reaction to the finding that communism left behind eighty-five million victims; to his conviction, even such a high number of innocent victims cannot tarnish communist ideals. Communism is capable of showing even the greatest evil as something innocent and pure. One can no longer be a Nazi after the Auschwitz, but after the gulags one can remain a communist with all innocence and purity. Besançon considers this the most powerful condemnation of communist ideology. The charm of communism is so strong that it prevents one to recognize a crime is a crime and induces one to see the worst evil as the highest good. "Every communist experience is repeated in innocence." (Besançon 2014, 64) Communism is perverted so radically that in spite of all its crimes it still appears to observers as innocent.

Solzhenitsyn has addressed the issue of violence from the historical perspective in his reflection *Live Not By Lies!* (1974). "And the simplest and most accessible key to our self-neglected liberation lies right here: Personal non-participation in lies. Though lies conceal everything, though lies embrace everything, but not with any help from me." "This opens a breach in the imaginary encirclement caused by our inaction." One does not actively create the delusions and lies, which give shelter to violence, but allows violence by tolerating lies. It is thus possible to deprive violence of its power by renouncing lie. "It is the easiest thing to do for us, but the most devastating for the lies. Because when people renounce lies, it simply cuts short their existence. Like an infection, they can exist only in a living organism." Lie gets its vital strength from human indecisiveness. How then to deprive lie of its vital strength? It is not necessary, says Solzhenitsyn, to march into the streets and squares and protest and publicly speak out what we think is truth. It suffices to "refuse to say that which we do not think." By renouncing lie, man protects his soul; if not, says Solzhenitsyn, man should not consider himself progressive and meritorious, and boast of his academic or artistic accomplishments. Path into freedom requires courage. The man who is not prepared to overcome his own fear should not complain about his un-freedom, which he has chosen; to him we can apply the words of Pushkin: "Why should cattle have the gifts of freedom? Their heritage from generation to generation is the belled yoke and the leash." (Solzhenitsyn 1974)

References

Besançon, A. 2014. *Zlo stoletja: o komunizmu, nacizmu in edinstvenosti judovskega holokavsta*. Ljubljana: Družina. Orig. publ. *Le malheur du siècle.* Paris: Fayard, 1998.

Clausewitz, C. von. 2000 [1832]. *Vom Kriege*. Munich: Cormoran.

Dürrenmatt, F. 1980 [1962]. *Die Physiker: Eine Komödie in zwei Akten*. Zurich: Diogenes.

Finkielkraut, A. 1996. *L'humanité perdue: essai sur le XXe siècle*. Paris: Editions du Seuil. Eng. trans. Judith Friedlander. *In the Name of Humanity: Reflections on the Twentieth Century*. New York: Columbia University Press, 2010.

Girard, R. 2007. *Achever Clausewitz*. Paris: Carnets nord. Eng. trans. Mary Baker. *Battling to the End: Conversations with Benoît Chantre*. East Lansing: Michigan State University Press, 2010.

Himmler, H. 2014. *Himmler privat: Briefe eines Massenmörders*. Munich: Piper.

Kierkegaard, S. 1909–. *Papirer.* 16 vol. Edited by V. Kuhr, E. Torsting, N. Thulstrup and N. J. Cappelørn. Kopenhagen: Gyldendal.

Levi, P. 1987. *Si c'est un homme.* Paris: Julliard.

Lévinas, E. 1976. *Difficile liberté.* Paris: Albin Michel.

Pascal, B. 1963. *Les provinciales.* In *Œuvres complètes,* 371–470. Paris: Seuil.

–––. 2003. *Pensées.* Trans. W. F. Trotter. Mineola, N.Y.: Dover Publications.

Solzhenitsyn, A. 1974. Live Not By Lies. *The Washington Post*, 18. 2, A26. Http://www.columbia.edu/cu/augustine/arch/solzhenitsyn/livenotbylies.html (accessed January 28, 2015).

HUMAN REFUSAL OF THE BASIC TRUTH ABOUT SELF AS THE ORIGIN OF VIOLENCE

Bojan Žalec, Ljubljana

"We would rather be ruined than changed
We would rather die in our dread
Than climb the cross of the moment
And let our illusions die".
(Auden 2011, 105)[1]

1. Introduction

The aim of this paper is to present one part of the work of the lucid and penetrating American thinker, theologian Charles K. Bellinger. He is original at interpreting and advancing the findings of Søren Kierkegaard, Eric Voegelin and René Girard.[2] This essay presents Bellinger's account of dangerous, harmful and violent pathological states and actions that originate in disturbances in three inseparably linked dimensions of human life: first, the vertical dimension, which consists of the relationship between a human and God; second, the temporal trajectory of development or non-development of the human self (the "I"); third, the horizontal or societal dimension. Bellinger founds his claims upon special theological anthropology, which in turn is grounded on Kierkegaard's findings that Bellinger interprets and applies to modern and contemporary phenomena. This forms the basis for establishing the link between human refusal to accept the basic truth about self and the violent character of his actions.

1 The famous poet Wystan Hugh Auden (1907-1973) should be mentioned as an important Bellinger's forerunner. Kierkegaard's influence on him was crucial. He developed – several decades earlier – considerably similar thoughts as Bellinger. I owe this knowledge to Martina Pavlíkova and Roman Králik's paper on Kierkegaard's influence on Auden's work that they presented in Škocjan on June 15, in the frame of the 5th Miklavž Ocepek symposium in Slovenia. See also Pavlíkova 2016.

2 About Bellinger's views on all three of them – and his application and development of their ideas - see Bellinger 2015, also Bellinger 2001; about Kierkegaard and Girard see Bellinger 2010.

Through this presentation I hope to show the fundamental importance and relevance of Søren Kierkegaard's (and other like thinkers as Eric Voegelin and René Girard) work, since it can help us understand that – and why – the roots of the modern world's central problems (like violence, terrorism, egocentric individualism etc.) cannot be understood without taking into account the theological or transcendental dimension of human beings, or in other words, theological or transcendental anthropology.[3] The aim of the essay is the presentation of Bellinger's understanding of origins of human deviant states which result in violence. Hence, I present Bellinger, and not Kierkegaard. It is true that many Kierkegaard's ideas function as Bellinger's starting points, and that Bellinger's thought is strongly pervaded with Kierkegaard's. Therefore, many true statements about Bellinger also apply to Kierkegaard. Anyway, in this essay Bellinger – not Kierkegaard - is in focus. In my earlier publications, I already presented some of Bellinger`s ideas, specifically his Kierkegaardin account of Nazism and Stalinism. (Žalec 2014 and 2015) In this essay, I will fill in another part to this picture, maybe more general strokes too.

Bellinger understands theological anthropology as an empirically oriented interpretation of observable personality types. (Bellinger 2015 (hereafter TS), loc. 2048-54) The essence of this approach is to apply the theological ideas to explain – or better to interpret – the observable human behaviour. He thinks that theological anthropology, and also theological psychology and political science, can compete with secular social and cultural science and humanities. Actually, such theological anthropology already exists. We can find examples in the works of Søren Kierkegaard, Eric Voegelin and René Girard. Their works, according to Bellinger, enable us to understand better human behaviour than their secular counterparts. Furthermore, Bellinger adds, the theological science – for which he argues – is not only more efficacious by explaining the data of human behaviour, but also better by showing to humanity an ethical path of living. It is better in this regard because it spells out the essential structure of human condition.

3 Here we should point also to other thinkers from 20th Century that share with Kierkegaard the view about the fatality of neglecting or refusing of transcendence (of man) and religion, or even hatred towards them. Besides Voegelin (his analysis and criticism of the "Gnosticism" of modernity) and Girarad, Pope John Paul II (2005) is one of the most relevant of them.

2. Dimensions of human existence and types of personality

Bellinger distinguishes three dimensions of human existence:

1. the vertical axis: God and nature,
2. the horizontal axis: social existence,
3. the temporal trajectory of individual selfhood.

These dimensions offer us a ground to understand three key thinkers who have given us a tool to understand human violence: Kierkegaard, Voegelin and Girard. Already in the beginning of his book *The Trinitarian Self* Bellinger offers to the reader a for-taste of his argument by listing three deviate types of personality: fundamentalist, individualist and revolutionary. Fundamentalists stress (only) the vertical axis and try to live in "God's pocket". Egocentric individualists focus on the self. Revolutionaries (such as Karl Marx) take into account the social plane and neglect the other two dimensions. All these views oversimplify the proper way to live in a complex world. On the other side, Bellinger thinks that our task is to live in the centre, in the intersection of all three dimensions and with the openness to the complexity that God calls us to participate in. Bellinger claims that what he tries to demonstrate is the thesis that the simplistic way of thinking should be replaced with the complex one. He is convinced that the person who relies only on one origin of knowledge – whether it is the Bible, or reason, or tradition, or experience – is not so intellectually advanced as the one who uses all the four. These four sources point to the four aspects of human life and if there are not included all four then we get a defective picture of reality, the human being and consecutively, the proper way of living.

Bellinger distinguishes four personal types regarding the three dimensions of reality as experienced by humans:

	A person refuses a continuous process of creation – and its uncertainty – in favour of a more static form of existence about which she/he thinks that she/he can control.		**A person accepts a continuous process of creation and she/he decides for a dynamic form of existence.**	
	1A	1B	2A	2B
emotional posture	passivity	self-assertiveness	arrogance	humility
psychological type	fundamentalist	individualist	utopian	maturing person
temporal centre of gravity	past	present	future	the fullness of time

Table 1: *Personal types* (TS, loc. 1584–1603)

The three dimensions are refracted in the Christian tradition in many different ways (including Kierkegaard's three spheres of existence). Thus, what Bellinger does is in a sense not original at all. What is original, however, as he himself says, is – firstly – his tenacity in how he notices and gathers together and connects these dimensions and refractions, and – secondly – how he applies them to the modern phenomena and events like Marxism, Stalinism, Nazism, modern individualism, fundamentalism, 9/11 etc. The three dimensions are lenses that enable us to see more clearly the roots of evil and violence. Bellinger wants to put the dimensions of the vertical, horizontal and the individual in one comprehensive and complex anthropological whole so that the picture of that whole, which is the real thing, would appear more clearly.

Usually it is said that Kierkegaard speaks about the stages of existence. For instance, Kierkegaard's book *Stadier paa Livets* is translated in English as *Stages on Life's Way*. Unfortunately, to translate *stadier* as *stages* suggests that Kierkegaard had in mind a developmental psychology account. But, this is not what he meant. These dimensions – the vertical (religious), the horizontal (ethical), and the temporal trajectory of life (aesthetic) are always with us. Therefore, it is better to speak about the spheres of existence or about "dimensions" of reality (as experienced by humans).

Kierkegaard`s opus, theses, viewpoints, accounts etc. are of course very demanding and complex and as such they represent a very hard exegetical task. This is evidenced by the fact that even capable interpreters who put great effort into the study of his texts may interpret Kierkegaard wrongly, and that we have so many opposite and even contradictory interpretations of Kierkegaard (for instance, for some he is a pro-fascist author[4], for others (like Bellinger) the most anti-fascist[5] etc.). Alas a more often praxis than hardworking study is what Bellinger calls a graffiti approach (TS, loc. 531–35 ff.). This means that the interpreter writes something about Kierkegaard that is not justified (at all) if we really study his work but that is somehow easy to remember or understand. A good example is "his" famous "leap of faith" about which maybe the first thing to know is that he never used this phrase. As stages of existence, you will find it in many encyclopaedias and other works. Neither should we forget to point out the pseudonymic aspect of Kierkegaard's opus. Kierkegaard once wrote that if his works are quoted they should be quoted by pseudonymic authors, not by his

4 Like György Lukacs (1969).
5 Bellinger 1992; 2001; 2010; Žalec 2014 and 2105.

name. And last but not least, we can discern several writing styles and authorships in Kierkegaard. Bellinger for instance, divides Kierkegaard's authorship into two time periods and six writing styles. (TS, loc. 478–90 ff.)

3. The roots of evil and the way to overcome them

An example of an unjustified but nevertheless very common criticism addressed to Kierkegaard is the accusation of individualism (on that basis he is evaluated as an unhelpful thinker).[6] But this is far from the truth because critics overlook important distinctions. They just stress that he argues in favour of the individual and that he refuses the crowd. What they neglect is his distinction between genuine sociality and crowd on one hand, and secondly, that he does not regard the individual as such as an end, but rather as a moment and a doorway to the genuine sociality. (TS, loc. 580–83) The crowd is human sociality in a corrupted form. It is a consequence of the mutiny against God and resistance to spiritual growth. To become a genuine individual, a single individual, is to leave this sphere and become a moment of positive spirituality marked by love of God, self and neighbour. (TS, loc. 580–91)

We can quote a rather large passage from *Works of Love* to support the above interpretation:

"Just as nowadays attempts are made in so many ways to emancipate people from all bonds, also beneficial ones, so also attempts are made to emancipate the emotional relationship between people from the bond that binds one to God and binds one in everything, in every expression of life. In connection with love, there is the desire to teach people something totally new, something for which the new old-fashioned Holly Scripture already has the characteristic expression – there is the desire to teach people the freedom that is 'without God in the world' ...

As a reward for such presumption, all existence will probably come closer and closer to being transformed into doubt or into a vortex in that way. What, after all, is the Law, what is the Law's requirement of a person? Well, that is for people to decide. Which people? Here doubt begins ... In order to have to begin to act, the individual must first find out from 'the others' what the Law's requirement is, but each one of these others must in turn as an individual find this out from 'the others'. In this way all human life transforms itself into one big excuse – is this perhaps the great, matchless common enterprise, the great

6 For the refusal of this reproach, see TS, loc. 570–72 ff.

achievement of the human race? The category 'the others' becomes fanciful, and the fancifully sought determination of what constitutes the Law's requirement is a false alarm ...

To what can we compare that confused state just described? Is it not a mutiny? Or should we hesitate to call it that if at a given time the whole human race was guilty of it and we then add, note well, that it is a mutiny against God? Or is morality subordinated to coincidence in this way: when a great number do what is wrong, or we all do it, then this wrong is the right? This explanation would in turn be nothing more than a repetition of the thinking of the mutiny or its thoughtlessness, because then ultimately is people who determine the Law's requirement instead of God. Therefore, the one who forgets this not only becomes personally guilty of rebellion against God but also contributes his share to the mutiny's gaining the upper hand ...

Only when all of us, each one separately receives his orders at one place, if I may put it this way, and then each one separately unconditionally obeys the same orders, only then substance and purpose and truth and actuality are in existence ... When this is the case, there is durability in existence because God has a firm hold on it. There is no vortex, because each individual begins, not with 'the others' and therefore not with evasions and excuses, but begins with the God-relationship and therefore stands firm and thereby also stops, as far as he reaches, the dizziness that is the beginning of mutiny." (Kierkegaard 1995, 114–18)

According to Bellinger, the description in this quotation corresponds quite clearly to the condition of the modern world that is characterized by the vertical mutiny against God and chaos as a consequence. The only way to overcome such a situation is that individuals alone directly establish a proper relationship with God and then unconditionally follow his commands. (TS, loc. 614–17)

Let us look at another passage from Kierkegaard, this time from his essay *On the Dedication to "That Single Individual"*:

"A crowd – not this or that, one now living or long dead, a crowd of the lowly or of nobles, of rich or poor, etc., but in its very concept – is untruth, since a crowd either renders the single individual wholly unrepentant and irresponsible, or weakens his responsibility by making it a fraction of his decision ... For every single individual who escapes into the crowd, and thus flees in cowardice from being a single individual, contributes his share of cowardice to 'the cowardice,' which is: the crowd. Take the highest, think of Christ – and the whole human race, all human beings, which were ever born and ever will be born; the situation is the single individual, as an individual, in solitary surroundings alone with him; as a single individual he walks up to him and spits on him: the human being has never been born and never will be, who would have the courage or the impudence for it; this is the truth. But since they remain in a crowd, they have the courage for it – what frightening untruth." (Kierkegaard 2011, 3-4)[7]

It is evident that Kierkegaard was very critical of the (social) relationships that grew from one's alienation to God. Bellinger points out that "Kierkegaard understood the world as a sphere of the creative activity of God." (TS, loc. 548-51) Kierkegaard took the claim about God's creation of the world and its beings through speech very seriously. As Bellinger expressed this Kierkegaard's view: "Everything that exists does so because God is speaking it into existence." (Ibid.) Bellinger's main point is that the central moment in Kierkegaard is the relationship between God and man, between God's call to man to grow, to become a self before God - a mature person who is motivated by faith, hope and love - and man's answer to this call. This growth or becoming involves pain. Humans react to this in different ways. Some of them try to avoid this pain and deafen themselves to the call. Kierkegaard calls such an attitude and a corresponding way of life a being to death.

Kierkegaard's view on the defections in the three dimensions is the following (TS, loc. 644–46):

1. the vertical dimension – mutiny against God;
2. selfhood – resistance to the call to growth;
3. the horizontal dimension - the crowd is untruth.

We can notice the interconnectedness – in Kierkegaard's thinking – of love for God, self and neighbour (TS, loc. 644–46 ff.). That we are all called by God to become a mature person who loves others is the central topic of *Works of Love* (TS, loc. 656–59). This work is an extended meditation on the creative speech of God (ibid.), which very concretely comes to us with the words of Jesus that we must love the other as we love ourselves. We can become an individual before God, a Self. This happens when we lift from the horizontal level (society) through development and growth of the individual self to God (the vertical axis). But, Kierkegaard is not a "Gnostic" who wants to leave the world. He returns back to the world where he tries to love his neighbour as himself. The individual who stands before God, the self, is motivated by faith, hope and love (loc. 678–80).

The process of the transformation to self can be described, according to Bellinger, by the Greek word *askesis* (loc. 680–83). Its original meaning was athletic training or practice, for instance training for the Olympics (loc. 680–83). Yet

7 This is Bellinger's own translation. Hongs' translation of the same essay is published in *The Point of View* under the title *For "That Single Individual"* (105-112).

in the early Christianity, the term was translated into the spiritual context and referred to exercises of monks and nuns for the purpose of greater openness to God. One of Kierkegaard's works is called *Practice in Christianity.* Bellinger points out that "the Danish term *Indøvelse*, translated as *practice*, or as *training* in the earlier edition, is the direct equivalent of *askesis*." (Loc. 683–692) He explains further:

"For Kierkegaard, spiritual growth is a Christological event. We become individuals before God by modelling ourselves after Christ, who is the prototype of true selfhood. When this point is not understood, critics interpret Kierkegaard's comments on 'the single individual' out of context and accuse him of 'individualism'. In reality, Kierkegaard's understanding of what it means to be individual *before God,* truly loving *the neighbor*, shows that the ultimate antidote for modern individualism is Christian *askesis*." (Ibid.)

The three aspects of reality and the questions connected with them – who is God, who are we, and what should we do – are mutually connected with bonds which cannot be broken. This means that we cannot separate one of them from the other two without starting the war against reality. If we try to comprehend ourselves as human beings without connection to God and ethics, then we end in insanity, like Nietzsche, to allege Bellinger's example (TS, loc. 2668–70). If we want to create an "ethical" society by refusing God and by denying of the sacredness of every human life, we end in insanity of Stalinism. If we want to be with God or to follow God but – on the other side – we refuse our self and we hate our neighbours, our fellow people, we end in insanity of 9/11 hijackers (TS, loc. 2670–73). A sin includes alienation from God, a resistance to the growth in self, and hatred against the fellow humans (TS, loc. 2621–24). When we comprehend the nature of these unbreakable bonds between the dimensions of reality then we find out that the principle "the aim consecrates the mean" is a philosophical mistake which originates in human psychopathology. There is no aim that could override the ethical since the ethical is inseparably connected with the authentic self and God's work of continuous creation (TS, loc. 2673–75).

4. Concluding remarks: the importance of religion or on the way to post-secular culture

Perhaps someone will find this paper sounding as a kind of fundamentalism. To such a reproach, I would answer: firstly, it is based on Kierkegaard. "Despite" his deep Christian faith, Kierkegaard did not ascribe to any label of fundamentalism, not if we take into account his sharp criticism of Christendom, crowd (as untruth), voluntary martyrdom (I don't have the right to be killed by others), his stressing of the importance of single individuality, etc. Moreover, the approach of theological anthropology presented here enables us to offer a convincing and coherent understanding of fundamentalism as a form of idolatry.

Secondly, everything that Bellinger writes and bases on Christian and other religious, theological and philosophical tradition, Kierkegaard, Voegelin, Girard etc., is not only compatible with the postsecular account, that I myself find both accurate and promising, but rather also a substantial contribution to it. Postsecularists do not consider secularisation as such as something bad but rather as in principle good. They accept (some) findings and values of the Enlightenment and in this respect the postsecular attitude can be seen even as its "continuation". But, on the other hand, postsecularists refuse all forms of shallow – and in a sense naive – secularism, which is contemptuous – or even hated and phobic – to the old wisdom and religion(s) and to the achievements of the presecular cultures. (Ošlaj 2015) If we truly want to cultivate peace, humanity, dialogue, respect for every human being, for the other (as the other) etc., we must learn (again) to appreciate transcendence, including the transcendence of both the human and the world. A good way to accomplish this, at least for many people, is through religious practices; however, a necessary way to "know" at least something about transcendence is to study religion(s) and the religious texts. So let me conclude with quotations of two eminent thinkers of our age. The first is from Luce Irigaray: "I recognize you means that I cannot know you in thought or in flesh." (Irigaray 2004, 8) The second is from Hans Küng - one of the most important theologians of our time and the founder of the World Ethos movement:

> "No peace among the nations
> without peace among the religions.
> No peace among the religions
> without dialogue between the religions.
> No dialogue between the religions
> without investigation of the foundation of the religions."
> (Küng 2007, xxiii)

These words have been - on one hand - quoted quite frequently but – on the other hand - rather neglected in social, political and economic decisions and practice, and – alas – even in scientific researches and study of the humanities. Let us hope that the situation will change. I have tried to contribute in a small way.

References

Auden, W. H. 2011. *The Age of Anxiety: A Baroque Eclogue*. Princeton: Princeton University Press.

Bellinger, Ch. K. 1992. Toward a Kierkegaardian Understanding of Hitler, Stalin, and the Cold War. In: George B. Connell and C. Stephen Evans (eds), *Foundations of Kierkegaard's Vision of Community: Religion, Ethics, and Politics in Kierkegaard*, New Jersey: Humanities Press, pp. 218-230. Reprinted in Bellinger 2010.

– – –. 2001. *The Genealogy of Violence: Reflection on Creation, Freedom and Evil.* New York: Oxford University Press.

– – –. 2010. *The Joker Is Satan and So Are We: And Other Essays on Violence and Christian Faith.* [S. l.]: CreateSpace Independent Publishing Platform.

– – –. 2015. *The Trinitarian Self: The Key to the Puzzle of Violence*. Edition Kindle.

Irigaray, L. 2004. *Key Writings*. London: Continuum.

Kierkegaard, S. 1988. *Stages on Life's Way.* Trans. Howard V. Hong. Princeton: Princeton University Press.

– – –. 1991. *Practice in Christianity.* Trans. Howard V. Hong. Princeton: Princeton University Press.

– – –. 1995. *Works of Love.* Trans. Howard V. Hong and Edna H. Hong. Princeton: Princeton University Press.

– – –. 2009³. For the Dedication to "That Single Individual". In: *The Point of View.* Trans. Howard V. Hong and Edna H. Hong. Princeton: Princeton University Press, pp. 105-112.

– – –. 2011. On the Dedication to "That Single Individual". In: Søren Kierkegaard, *Selected Essays*. Trans. Charles K. Bellinger & L. M. Hollander. Oxford: Benediction Classics, pp. 3-4. Available also on the Internet, in: http://www.ccel.org./ccel/kierkegaard/untruth/files/untruth.html (January 15, 2016)

Küng, H. 2007. *Islam, Past Present & Future*. Oxford: Oneworld Publications.

Lukács, G. 1969. *Razkroj uma: pot iracionalizma od Schellinga do Hitlerja.* Trans. Taras Kermauner (ger. original *Die Zerstörung der Vernunft*). Ljubljana: Cankarjeva založba.

Ošlaj, B. 2015. *Človek, svet in etos: študije o postsekularni filozofiji in svetovnem etosu* (Man, world and ethos: studies about postsecular philosophy and world ethos). Ljubljana: Znanstvena založba Filozofske fakultete.

Pavlíkova, M. 2016. The concept of anxiety and its reflection in Auden's work "The Age of Anxiety". *European Journal of Science and Theology*, 12(4): 111-119.

Pope John Paul II. 2005. *Memory & Identity: Personal Reflections.* London: Weidenfeld & Nicolson.

Žalec, B. 2014. Nazism and Stalinism in the light of Kierkegaard's thought. *Filozofia* 69(5): 443-450. Reprinted in Žalec 2015, pp. 39-47.

–––. 2015. *Genocide, Totalitarianism and Multiculturalism: Perspectives in the Light of Solidary Personalism*. Zürich & Berlin: Lit.

"HE DESCENDED INTO HELL": PEDAGOGICAL AND PSYCHOLOGICAL DIMENSION OF TRUTH AND COMPASSION

Stanko Gerjolj, Ljubljana

In the Apostolic Creed, before his resurrection, Jesus takes us "before Hell". This path is often set off by educators, counsellors and psychotherapists, when they emphatically entirely approach the "Hell of untruth and lies", in which there are people who are seeking help. Based on "Hell", Communism wanted to create "Heaven", which like the Tower of Babel began to tear down with the fall of the Berlin Wall, in these burnt areas, there are still many areas where wars are raging and tensions prevailing. Even in the Slovenian region, there are still strong waves of smoke billowing from the burnt area.

A key dimension in the quest for truth is a compassionate empathy with both the perpetrators of "Hell" as well as with those who was pushed into it. In "Hell", the truth is in fact misrepresented while people are silent or not allowed to speak about the real truth. Compassionate empathy enables a breakthrough to experiential truth, which in itself opens the way towards the actual truth. In a hellish period of Communism, there were many hidden truths, even between parents and children. Selective silence harms honest communication rather than a direct lie. We have learned to carry this "silence of the truth" from one generation to another. Significant changes have led us in a context where the path to – experiential and objective – truth is increasingly opening up. But along the way, we will certainly meet "before Hell". We can only hope that we travel with enough compassion and empathy to find a way of hope in a different, more "redeemed" and liberated future.

Trauma, truth and compassion

Atrocities have a lasting traumatic consequence for both carriers of such atrocities as well as for their victims. The perpetrators are afraid to face their truth as the latter would expose and "destroy" them. It would ruin not only their face, but also a big part of life, as it would reveal the nonsense of their actions. That is why they prefer to prolong their agony, though they often suspect that sooner or later everything will be revealed. The victims have suffered such severe trauma that it is impossible for them to talk about it and are accompanied by the feeling that they cannot convert it to words. At the same time, they are accompanied by fear of excessive proximity of traumatic events, which would have pushed them "before the Hell" again, into emotional reliving. They are often accompanied by the fear of misunderstanding and even condemning, as the propaganda machine of committed atrocities was so strong that it puts them more in the role of perpetrators than victims. They often resort to this overthrow themselves, since only this role allows them to survive. But, the path to truth is possible only through compassion, which creates conditions for contextualization and biographical-experiential dimensions of traumatic events in the eyes of both the perpetrators as well as the victims.

Generations after World War II

After the end of World War II, the winners celebrated and taunted over losers. Indeed, they felt as winners only when they after the end of the war finally "dealt" with their domestic opponents. This very fact alone suggests that their win was not as pure as they wish to display it. The losers were already from the time of the war largely familiar with brutality related plans of the communists and have therefore withdrawn, where possible or have emigrated. Almost all of them who failed to succeed in this, have experienced torture and killings and thereby the loss of their loved ones. In doing so, it is always important to keep in mind that – in conjunction with the communist ideology – in the vast majority of cases it was not about torture and killing of those who could in any way make them be accused or blamed of anything. The communists tortured and killed those who, with their very existence, represented a potential threat to their totalitarian regime. Therefore, many completely innocent people, often the whole families, including children and mothers, were tortured and killed.

Following such atrocities, both perpetrators as well as their victims suffer traumatic consequences. In both groups, the suicides were not uncommon. The perpetrators most commonly "overcome" their trauma by substantiating them with "higher goals" in the sense "the end justifies the means", while the fanatically cling to the maintenance of the totalitarian regime, which is the logical consequence of atrocities. Victims usually do not speak about the atrocities and, in particular with the future generations, hide and deny them from the fear of further possible consequences of totalitarianism, while completely surrendering to their work. In the fear of further consequences, they often even support totalitarianism and become a manageable mass and an excellent workforce, allowing the existence of totalitarianism. At constant ideological propaganda, in particular the following generation over time start to feel really guilty. They compensate these feelings by becoming even more directly involved in the maintenance of totalitarianism. It is a mechanism that puts the victim in a total dependency thus creating a sense of inferiority in them. The more the totalitarianism pushes an innocent victim to a corner, the more is such victim willing to listen and obey, and to support the perpetrator in a total subordination. (Verginella 2003, 185) This has also occurred because there was no natural and genuine communication between parents and their children (Bohleber 2009, 110). Murderers failed to tell their children about the atrocities because they did not want to show their real faces, while the victims have been hiding their feelings both out of fear of the regime as from a desire not to hurt their children. In most cases, the pain was so terrible that they were not able to talk about it. They distanced from the traumatic events and pushed them into the subconscious, since it was only this attitude that allowed them to survive.

Fear and silence

Even in an open and democratic environment, the victims of the atrocities are for a long time not able to speak of their suffering and pain (Jurić Pahor 2004, 52). In totalitarianism, which justifies its existence in practice by creating fear, this silence is even more obvious and understandable. By being silent, parents usually try to protect the next generations from the pain. In fact, with such silence being present, children feel the pain of their parents, sometimes even more than in cases where it is verbalized (Rosenthal 1999, 71).

Silence doesn`t constitute a "non-communication", but communicates the pain in a different way (Jurić Pahor 2004, 53), pulling the next generation into identification with the victims (Wutti 2013, 47-48). Especially in an environment that is imbued with fear, the victims often transform their unspoken pain into other forms of reliving and unique repetition, particularly in relation to children. Excessive fear, for example that the children are cold and will catch a cold or will consume some spoiled food, as well as the constant fear of disease, are frequent forms of traumatic repetition of own non-verbalized and unprocessed pain (Rosenthal 1999, 71). In conjunction with such forms of transformed expression of feelings, the victims often "easily" fail to detect any hint of their own pain, though they are convinced that they are not talking about it (Grünberg 2002, 40). In any case, children "know everything" about the traumatic pain of their parents, but since this is communicated by silence and repetition, they, in the sentient identification, often upgrade it with their own imagination (Rosenthal 1999, 71). On the one hand, we can partly console ourselves that "time heals wounds", while on the other hand, it is certainly also true that pain is transmitted from generation to generation and is becoming even stronger in the process. In this way, an excessive concern for children and fears of diseases and the like keep developing in parents in the later generations. Paradoxically, in these fears there also lies the fact that children may actually become sicklier and thus satisfy their parents that they were not afraid in vain. Still, such cases are usually only about fragmentary narratives. Pure confession would hurt too much, since it would only bring traumatic events closer, resulting in painful reliving (Klüger 2007, 139). However, the victims often sensed that traumatic feelings and pain cannot be put into words (Waynryb 2001, 111). It is also important to know that under Communism, even after atrocities, there was a realistic possibility that the victim, who would "say too much", would later experience new traumatic violence.

Trauma after the fall of Communism

Parallel to the traumatisation of pain there is a process of trauma collectivization, taking place on an individual level in the following generations, where children intuitively feel and connect, and thus form a kind of "we-feeling". In the communist totalitarianism, the collectivization of pain was certainly maintained and strengthened, and eventually became so strong that – with inclusion of many other problems of the communist regime – it led to political and social changes. Empowerment of victims was apparently also perceived in the descendants of communists, which convinced many of them to pragmatically change their mind and cross to the other side.

This is a similar path as the one walked upon by the descendants of victims during totalitarianism. Out of fear of the consequences, many of the descendants of the victims at that time pragmatically joined supporters of totalitarianism. At the same time, they did not entirely suppress the sense of which "we-group" they actually belong. As holders of authority and power, the communists easily implemented this seeming transformation. How false and pragmatic it really was, was showed in fact by almost all former communist societies as they in most cases held political power and – more or less successfully, in this sense, there are some differences – tried to re-establish it into the most similar systems, as they were in force prior to the amendments.

This is also often contributed by the victims, who have become accustomed to be quiet and still feel the fear of the confessing the truth. It is difficult for them to free themselves from the feelings of "guilt", despite the fact that they are victims (Rowland-Klein 2004, 122–130). Even though this hurts them, they agree to the adulterated truth, which dishonour the post-war killings and tortures, because this makes them feel less "guilty" in this conglomerate of interpretations (Silbermann and Stoffers 2000, 125). The future will certainly keep opening the wounds and allow for genuine confessions. In particular, the discovery of graves of communist atrocities, where the bones of those killed "receive meat and begin to talk" (Ez 37,7–10), evokes traumatic memories that this place needs in order for catharsis to occur (Dežman 2014, 616). Facing the pain thus opens the way to a “new life”, which the pain and the pressures cannot suppress (Jurić Pahor 2004, 43–44).

Traumas of victims and their truth

Unlike the traumatic consequences of Nazism and Fascism, which at least at the formal level could begin being processed relatively quickly after their downfall, such processes, after the fall of Communism, became even more complex and demanding? Even after the fall of Nazism and Fascism, where political changes took place faster after the atrocities than in Communism, the victims for a long time have not been able to cope with the endured trauma. While in Communism, the victims have been forced to remain silent for decades after the atrocities took place and in addition, they have been further subjected to constant pressure.

Following the fall of Nazism and Fascism, the cultural and artistic activities, which have opened the wounds of the past and supported their processing, relatively quickly developed the wounds of the past and supported their processing. After the fall of Communism, in most of the countries and especially in Slovenia, we hardly find any move in this area still having no effect on the collective consciousness.

Forced silence will certainly not heal the pain. The victims have “dislocated” it from their memory and lived as if “it” never happened. However, they have always bared the pain with themselves and sensed it as some kind of “foreign object in the soul”, constantly forcing the memory towards a confession (Klüger 2007, 139). It is a feeling triggered by any foreign object in the body: until it does not hurt, I can live as I do not have it; but when it hurts, I feel the need for its removal or confession. But, even after removal the foreign object remains a part of me and cannot be erased from the memory.

Perhaps the forced silence contributed somewhat to the fact that today the victims and their descendants see the traumatic events from a slightly greater distance, which helps them not to experience them so directly and tragically (Jurić Pahor 2004, 53). Nevertheless, the traumatic past is still catching up with us and is present among us. A wounded man stays wounded and even after confession or “liberation”, remains connected with pain (Pahor 1967, 25). However, if the pain remains unexpressed, then it keeps generating, collectivizing and growing from one generation to the next. Confession, of course, heals the pain mainly in generations, which have not experienced it directly. However, the research found that a trauma is “processed” only in the third (Wutti 2013, 51–52), sometimes even in the fourth or fifth generation (Jurić Pahor 2004, 55). Children of traumatized parents are marked by pain even before birth since the mother passes her feelings already to her unborn child (Verny and Kelly 1995, 45–54), which the child then experiences as if those happened to him. Only by narrating from generation to generation, these painful feelings decrease.

An additional difficulty in processing communist trauma is also in the fact that the communist totalitarianism lasted very long, over generations. If in fact the victim, during confession, remembers the life before the traumatic experience, he or she intuitively passes to children the message that there is also a different life. The vast majority of generations did not receive this message, because confessions were not enabled. This means that they were born in the shadow of Communism, in a sense, directly into the trauma and pain, which means that at a depth, they have no experience of non-traumatized life. In this context, generations, which in many cases are already grandparents, "hunt" the last opportunities to discover life "before the trauma". We can hope though that the democratic processes triggered a sufficient number of timely confessions, which allow that in conjunction with the processing of trauma, a new, non-traumatized life is also disclosed. Indeed, we must assume that based on the confession of directly traumatized parents, their children respond empathetically and optimistically enough to find vital force for positive messages in themselves, with which they liberate their children and grandchildren. In this case, namely the future generations will be able to attain the truths that are painful, but will not burden them in such a way that they would have to keep repeating them.

Pain, compassion and truth

On the one hand, pain is something that we do not want in life, while on the other hand, we are attracted to it empathetically. Compassion knows how to pull us into the pain of another. This is particularly true in the case of mental disability. In cases of communist atrocities, expressing pain was prohibited over many generations. Nevertheless, almost all the generations of victims felt this pain, and some of them even in potentiated form. Although public opinion was not favourable to that, a number of historians, publicists and others tackled to explore the life of their ancestors. In the vast majority, it was about exploring the life of the victims. The very research of "forbidden pain" gives hope that the pain can also be processed (Jurić Pahor 2004, 54).

If the first attempts were about the research with the purpose of rehabilitation of victims, which is quite relevant argument, since the majority of victims were innocent, the willingness to contextualize the understanding of atrocities is increasingly coming to the forefront. This does not mean justifying actions, however it expresses openness to emotional understanding of the time and the circumstances in which the atrocities occurred. Although the creators of public opinion are still caught up in some of the levers of a totalitarian past, despite this fact more and more people keep appearing, who open themselves to the truth. It is true that the process is slow but real facts, however, are coming to light and no darkness can conceal them completely. In this case is also good to know that the word is not everything. The creative media such as film, theatre, drawing or painting, often communicate more truth than the word (Kogan 2004, 109–111).

In disclosing the truth, the capability of empathy and compassion is of key importance. The victim will only then be able to withdraw from the role of "perpetrator", when such person receives compassion. At that time, both the victim and the perpetrator will be open to the truth. The truth in this case will become a "biography" and will no longer be just a plain fact. In the event of biographical truths that we accept with compassion, forgiveness both at the individual and collective level will no longer be a problem. This is, namely, about the question of how future generations will preserve the collective memory of the communist atrocities. When with compassion imbued various individual biographical memories will be able to be transformed into a "cultural memory", then the experience of both the perpetrators and victims can impact on the historical consciousness that such acts are not repeated (Rüsen 2001, 243).

References

Bohleber, W. 2009. Wege und Inhalte transgenerationaler Weitergabe: Psychoanalytische Perspektiven. In: H. Radebold, W. Bohleber, J. Zinnecker (eds.). *Transgenerationale Weitergabe kriegsbelasteter Kindheiten: Interdisziplinäre Studien zur Nachhaltigkeit historischer Erfahrungen über vier Generationen.* Weinheim – München: Juventa Verlag, pp. 107–118.

Dežman, J. 2014. Preseganje travmatskih bremen titoizma. *Bogoslovni vestnik*, 74: 611–638.

Jurić-Pahor, M. 2004. Neizgubljivi čas: travma fašizma in nacionalsocializma v luči nuje po "obdobju latence" in transgeneracijske transmisije. *Razprave in gradivo: Revija za narodnostna vprašanja*, 44: 38–64.

Klüger, R. 2007. *Weiter Leben: Eine Jugend.* München: DTV.

Kogan, I. 2004. Trauma, Resistenz und Kreativität: Beobachtungen aus Analysen von Kindern Holocaustüberlebender. In: M. Frölich, Y. Lapid, C. Schneider (eds.). *Repräsentationen des Holocaust im Gedächtnis der Generationen: Zur Gegenwartsbedeutung des Holocaust in Israel und Deutschland.* Frankfurt am Main: Brandes & Apsel.

Pahor, B. 1967. *Nekropola.* Maribor –Trst: Založba Obzorja – Založništvo tržaškega tiska.

Rosenthal, G. 1999. *Der Holocaust im Leben von drei Generationen: Familien von überlebenden der Shoah und von Nazi-Tätern.* Gießen: Psychosozial-Verlag.

Rowland-Klein, D. 2004. The transmission of trauma across generations: Identification with parental trauma in children of Holocaust survivors. In: D. R. Catherall (ed.). *Handbook of stress, trauma, and family.* New York: Brunner-Routledge, pp. 117–136.

Rüsen, J. 2001. Holocaust, Erinnerung, Identität. In: H. Welzer (ed.). *Das soziale Gedächtnis: Geschichte, Erinnerung, Tradierung.* Hamburg: Hamburger Edition, pp. 243–259.

Silbermann, A. & Stoffers, M. 2000. *Auschwitz: Nie davon gehört? Erinnerungen und Vergessen in Deutschland.* Berlin: Rowohlt.

Verginella, M. 2003. Primo Levi, razlagalec lagerske asimetrije. In: P. Levi. *Potopljeni in rešeni.* Ljubljana: Studia humanitatis, pp. 171–193.

Verny, T. & Kelly, J. 1995. *Das Seelenleben des Ungeborenen.* Frankfurt am Main – Berlin: Ullstein.

Waynryb, R. 2001. *The Silence: How tragedy shapes talk.* Crows Nest NSW (Australia): Allen & Unwin.

Wutti, D. 2013. Transgeneracijski prenosi v družinah koroških Slovencev. *Razprave in gradivo: Revija za narodnostna vprašanja*, 70: 45–54.

TRUTH, JUSTICE, UPRIGHTNESS: HUMAN FLOURISHING IN PROPHETIC PERSPECTIVE

Marcel V. Măcelaru, Bucharest and Timişoara

I

The idea of human flourishing is present across cultures (Selin and Davies 2012) and in most disciplines of human knowledge (Atherton, Graham, et al. 2011); and that with good reason. Although the terminology itself has only been around since Elizabeth Anscombe's (1958) use of "flourishing" in relation to Aristotle's *eudaimonia*, it is safe to assume that the ideals of wellbeing and happiness the concept evokes have had a much longer history – perhaps as long as humanity itself. Admittedly, opinions on what a flourishing life consists of and how it can be attained vary. In most definitions (cf. Volf 2015b, 132–133), "human flourishing" accounts for: emotional fulfilment (a life that *feels good*; e.g. Francis 2011); good health combined with material, professional, social and cultural contentment (a life that *goes well*; e.g. Bolt 2013); or excellence in terms of one's accomplishments (a life that is *lived well*; e.g. Wariboko 2009). True flourishing, nevertheless, will bring all these facets of wellbeing together; for, as Miroslav Volf (2015b, 133) observes, "life is truly and fully good [only] when (1) it goes well, (2) we lead it well, and (3) when it is pleasurable."

Within Christian circles, philosopher Nicholas Wolterstorff (2008; cf. also Wolterstorff 2005) has tied "human flourishing" to the biblical concept of *shalom*. In his view, to live a flourishing life is to live in right relationship with God, with neighbour, with creation and with self. Similarly, Adrian Thatcher (2011, 257) insists that,

> [f]or Christians, happiness is emphatically not the goal of life; nor is their account of right and wrong determined by the fallible calculation of felicific consequences. The meaning of life is rather to be found in the love of God, of one's neighbour, of one's self, and even of one's enemy.

Evidently, these represent a notable departure from the typical association of "flourishing" with pleasure, fulfilment and satisfaction. There is a clear implication in both views that "flourishing" is dependent on spiritual wellness; and as such, not everyone will ultimately flourish. Although all human beings bear, in a sense, the image of God, it is only when living life as God intended it, in harmonious conscientious relationship with the divine, that the potential to be fully human, that is, the potential to truly flourish, is unleashed. As the Creator, Ruler and Sustainer of all things, the triune God is necessarily the source of all "flourishing". Consequently, it is only by drawing closer to God that we are gradually transformed into his likeness and are empowered to live life to its fullness, uninhibited by sin, filled with meaning and crowned with gladness. Following from this, we may conclude then that "God's relation to human beings and human beings' relation to God [is] the condition of possibility for human life and flourishing in all dimensions" (Volf 2015a, 9).

II

It should be clarified, however, that the inclusion of spiritual wellness in this definition of "human flourishing" is neither a rehearsal of the "happiness hypothesis's" contention that religious values and participation in religion bring enduring levels of happiness (e.g. Layard 2005; cf. Haidt 2006) nor an assertion regarding Christianity's contribution to wellbeing (q.v. Atherton 2014, 62–102). Although both points have value, the "spirituality" in view here is not a reference to "religion". As Richard Stivers (1994, 64) rightly notes, "when religion is associated with happiness it is reduced to the status of a *means* (emphasis in original) to the end of happiness" – clearly the kind of instrumentalisation of faith that would justify Karl Marx's (1844, 71; cf. Marx 1976, 378) famous assertion: ""Die Religion ... ist das Opium des Volkes".[1] Rather, what I have in view is *a mode of existence that is markedly theological* – an existence which necessitates the adoption of a biblically-grounded world-view and pertains to the experience of relational (covenantal) fullness the life lived correspondingly guarantees (cf. Zizioulas 1985).

In calling such existence "theological", I take my clue from Karl Barth, who has defined "theology" as "the commerce and communion between God and man" (Barth 1967, 9; q.v. Măcelaru 2014). The implication of Barth's definition is that the existence described here as "theological" entails divine-human interaction (commerce) within the context of divine-human fellowship (communion). Consequently, "human flourishing" concerns a dynamic, relational involvement with God; that is, when seen in this way, "human flourishing" is nothing less than ""life with God".

1 Regrettably, regarding the atheist critique of religion, Kirk (1992) has concluded that much of what Marx, Nietzsche and Freud attacked in religion actually deserved to be attacked.

Nonetheless, the definition of "human flourishing" suggested here is clearly holistic, for "life with God" impinges on all dimensions of Christian experience and praxis: the private, the ecclesial and the public. To explain, in practical terms, such theological existence translates into personal endeavour, whereby an *individual experience* of God is in view. It refers to what one does in order to connect, and live out a relationship, with God. This also translates into ecclesial endeavour, whereby a *collective experience* of God is in view. It refers to what one does as a member of a community of faith, in pursuit of a shared relational knowledge of the divine. And, it translates into public endeavour, whereby the *societal implications* of one's relationship with God are in view. This refers to the covenantal role one has of being a blessing for the other. Such an existence, then, requires the broadening of the typically limited perspective on religion, within which Christian faith is perceived as a private Sunday-practiced Church-bound affair, toward a holistic understanding of Christian spirituality as an existence that integrates faith with all dimensions of life: the spiritual, the physical, the intellectual, the emotional, the aesthetic and the social. Consequently, such a pursuit of "human flourishing" becomes a quest for a holistic development of personhood, with all that it entails: identity development in light of one's quality of being part of a social nexus (cf. McFadyen 1990).

III

The introduction of "personhood" as a category in this discussion helps explain that "life with God" is a transformational journey, a process of becoming Christ-like within which relational revelation takes place. It is a life characterized by ordered continuity and dynamism (process), in which one's identity is shaped towards fulfilling the divine vision for humanity (becoming Christ-like), as s/he grows from knowing *of* and *about* God, with an emphasis on the intellect, toward *knowing God*, with an emphasis on covenant (relational revelation).

The roots of such a view on personhood are to be found in the assertion that humans are created in the "image and likeness" of God (Gen. 1:26). Expectably, the interpretation of this phrase has caught the attention of various interpreters over the years (on this, see further Măcelaru 2011, 55-56). This history notwithstanding, the reference in the same context to Adam, who sires a "son in his own likeness, in his own image" (Gen. 5:3), together with Luke's depiction of Adam as the "son of God" (Lk. 3:38) clearly imply the relational dimension noted above. God, who is a relational being, creates mankind to reflect that relationality. As such, personhood is fully understandable only in light of humanity's relationship with the Divine Being.

To be sure, each individual is significant on his/her own, for each is created in the image and likeness of God and each is expected to grow into Christ-likeness. However, the creation account makes it clear that it is mankind, comprising man and woman, that reflects the divine. As such, there is an emphasis on a communal rather than an individual stance as well, for neither man nor woman can alone fulfil the divine purpose. Thus, personhood, in the biblical thought, refers to humans as entities that are in relationship with God and with other humans. Applied to the task at hand, this view on personhood indicates that there is a *social dimension* to human flourishing. One cannot flourish on his/her own, for as a social category, flourishing necessarily "depends upon passion for and commitment to the common good" (Brueggemann 2011, 19).

Nonetheless, even then, the idea that individuals are being formed and shaped by the relational encounters they experience is not complete; that is, it does not reflect accurately the view of the creation account unless the relational nexus defining personhood also includes mankind's relationship to the created world. The story of the creation shows clearly that, as relational beings, expected to relate in a specific way, humans are under the obligation to further divine purposes. Specifically, the "job" of humankind is to ensure the well-being of God's entire creation. Consequently, reflecting the divine in this context means more than the capacity humans have for community. It is in fact the extension of God's perfect order over the entire creation.

Undoubtedly, such mode of existence, that is, the flourishing implied in the biblical view of such covenantal living, when faced with the realities of our day by day living, appears lofty and unattainable. Nevertheless, as Brueggemann (2011, 28) explains, such "'[f]lourishing' is not a given; but it is made chooseable". That is, it is made chooseable by the poetic emancipatory imagination available in the Bible. Admittedly, the Bible does not speak of human flourishing *per se*. However, it offers plenty in terms of such poetic imagination, which, when engaged, ushers in the divine alternative of a "world haunted by the spirit of truth." To this end, I propose to conclude this discussion on human flourishing by "engaging", at least minimally, the Biblical world of "poetic imagination". Such evoking, Brueggemann (2011, 28) urges, is "a fundamental precondition for a society that can flourish". Thus, the hermeneutical downpayment below.

IV

The passage I offer is Jeremiah's call to truth, justice and uprightness, which reads as follows:

> If you swear, "As the Lord lives!" in truth, in justice, and in uprightness, then nations shall be blessed by him, and by him they shall boast (Jer. 4:2).

The prophecy of Jeremiah addresses a people for which cruelty, idolatry, social injustice and selfishness had become common patterns of behaviour. For the most part, its message is a stark warning that God's punishment for such failures will be swift and inescapable. Nothing short of wholesale repentance would suffice in order to address the rampant sinfulness of the nation and prevent this proximate doom. Like all true Israelite prophets, Jeremiah envisions such repentance as the restoration within the community of moral and social values that would match Israel's covenantal obligations. Everything that did not befit that identity, all social, political, economic and religious realities that were incongruent with Israel's theological discourse, were to be eliminated in order for the nation to become engaged once again in the concreteness of covenantal ethical living. To that end, Jeremiah calls the Israelites to renewed dedication to the divine–human relationship, that being the only way to restore the nation to its destiny of being a blessing to all peoples announced in the Abrahamic covenant that is, the restoration of human–human relationship; and also the only way to ensure their continuity in the Promised Land, that is, the manifestation of rightness in the human–creation relationship.

Within this larger thematic context, the passage in view offers God's solution to the problematic realities confronting the Israelite society. Its purpose is to lead back this people to a place of rightness, to *shalom.* This is the place where their God-given destiny would be fulfilled; it is the place of true flourishing. The path the Israelites are to follow, the prophecy makes this unequivocally clear, starts with the embrace of "truth". Within the Old Testament, with reference to human beings, truth is the quality that gives validity and legitimacy to one's claims and therefore to one's life. With reference to God, "truth" is but another way of speaking of divine utterances – it is the sum of all God's commandments and all God's promises. It is ultimately a reference to God's very being. As such, to choose "truth" would be a return to the foundational awareness of all that is good and right in terms of the divine–human relationship. It is the propositional content of a theological mode of existence, the ontological dimension of human flourishing.

Furthermore, the Israelites are to do "justice". As with truth, justice is also a quality that applies to both God and humans. It is the way God acts, for it reflects God's very nature. But, it is also the way humans should act among themselves, for the divine behaviour sets standards of conduct for all God's people. It is in fact the primary guideline for interpersonal behaviour, for only by acting justly they can ensure the rule of fairness and honesty within the community. As such, justice here refers to the active implementation of truth – an encompassing description of relating rightly to one another. This is the social aspect of a theological mode of existence and the deontological dimension of human flourishing.

Finally, the Israelites are to live in "uprightness". This is a term which refers to unchanging standards, correctness, genuineness, and forthrightness. Such is the way God's holiness is explained in the Old Testament. Furthermore, such is the way God's holy people ought to be. Uprightness is the rule of behaviour Israelites are to follow, for wholeness and integrity are only found in the total application of God's law, both at personal and at societal levels. The promise of such living is: healthy relationships, characterized by genuine openness, humility, generosity and lack of deceitful calculations. Thus, uprightness impinges on the entire relational nexus defining individuals and communities. It is the covenantal framework, within which the embrace of truth and the doing of justice take place. Uprightness is the relational context within which humans and their communities will operate, that is, will flourish, as intended by the Creator.

Evidently, this interpretation emphasizes Jeremiah's call to renewal as a pursuit for right relations. This is a justified reading in the light of the fact that the sin of Israel, in the larger context of the book, pertains to broken relationships caused by social injustice and inequality. It is therefore no surprise that the solution offered by God through the prophet urges every member of the community to be actively involved in relationship reparation. This message, I suggest, is as relevant within our contexts as it was for the people of Jeremiah's time. The vision of society offered here (and elsewhere in the Bible), if appropriated, can lead to true flourishing. It can lead to *shalom*, for the divine "map" of right relationships provided in Jeremiah's prophecy guides to harmonious covenantal living with God, with neighbour and with creation.

References

Anscombe, G.E.M. 1958. Modern Moral Philosophy. *Philosophy*, 33(124): 1–16.

Atherton, J. 2014. *Challenging Religious Studies: The Wealth, Wellbeing and Inequalities of Nations.* London: SCM Press.

Atherton, J., Graham, E., and Steedman, I. (eds). 2011. *The Practices of Happiness: Political Economy, Religion and Wellbeing.* London: Routledge.

Barth, K. 1967. *The Humanity of God.* Fontana Library of Theology and Philosophy. London: Collins.

Bolt, J. 2013. *Economic Shalom: A Reformed Primer on Faith, Work and Human Flourishing.* Grand Rapids, MI: Christian's Library Press.

Brueggemann, W. 2011. Prophetic Imagination Toward Social Flourishing. In: M. Higton, C. Rowland and J. Law (eds), *Theology and Human Flourishing:*

Essays in Honor of Timothy J. Gorringe. Eugene, OR: Wipf and Stock Publishers, pp. 16–30.

Haidt, J. 2006. *The Happiness Hypothesis: Putting Ancient Wisdom and Philosophy to the Test of Modern Science*. London: Arrow Books.

Kirk, J.A. 1992. *Loosening the Chains: Religion as Opium and Liberation*. London: Hodder and Stoughton.

Layard, R. 2005. *Happiness: Lessons from a New Science*. London: Allen Lane.

Marx, K. 1844. Zur Kritik der Hegel`schen Rechtsphilosophie. In: Arnold Ruge and K. Marx (eds), *Deutsch-Französische Jahrbücher*. Paris: Bureau der Jahrbücher, pp. 71–85.

Marx, K. 1976. Zur Kritik der Hegelschen Rechtsphilosophie. In: *Marx-Engels-Werke, Bd. 1*. Berlin: Dietz Verlag, pp. 378–91.

Măcelaru, M.V. 2011. Examples to Follow, Imperatives to Obey: On the "Father" Metaphor for God and Its Implications. *Plērōma* 13: 55–56.

Măcelaru, M.V. 2014. Theology Encounters Globalization. *European Journal of Science and Theology* 10(1): 67–78.

McFadyen, A.I. 1990. *The Call to Personhood: A Christian Theory of the Individual in Social Relationships*. Cambridge: Cambridge University Press.

Selin, H. & Davies, G. (eds). 2012. *Happiness Across Cultures: Views of Happiness and Quality of Life in Non-Western Cultures*. London: Springer.

Stivers, R. 1994. *The Culture of Cynicism: American Morality in Decline*. Oxford: Blackwell.

Thatcher, A. 2011. Theology, Happiness, and Public Policy. In: M. Higton, C. Rowland and J. Law (eds), *Theology and Human Flourishing: Essays in Honor of Timothy J. Gorringe*. Eugene, OR: Wipf and Stock Publishers, pp. 251–64.

Volf, M. 2015a. *Flourishing: Why We Need Religion in a Globalized World*. New Haven, NY: Yale University Press.

Volf, M. 2015b. The Crown of the Good Life: A Hypothesis. In: M. Volf and J.E. Crisp (eds), *Joy and Human Flourishing: Essays on Theology, Culture and the Good Life*. Minneapolis, MN: Fortress Press, pp. 127–36.

Wariboko, N. 2009. *The Principle of Excellence: A Framework for Social Ethics*. Plymouth: Lexington Books.

Wolterstorff, N. 2005. *Educating for Shalom: Essays on Christian Higher Education*. Grand Rapids, MI: Eerdmans.

Wolterstorff, N. 2008. God's Power and Human Flourishing. Available on-line at: <http://faith.yale.edu/sites/default/files/nicholas_wolterstorff_-_gods_power_and_human_ flourishing_0.pdf>. Accessed on: 10 October 2015.

Zizioulas, J.D. 1985. *Being as Communion: Studies in Personhood and the Church*. Crestwood, NY: St Vladimir's Seminary Press.

TRUTH AND COMPASSION – HUMAN DIGNITY, THE ETHICAL NORM WHICH SHOULD BE RESPECTED BY ALL PERSONS

Anton Jamnik, Ljubljana

World ethos – life as something sacred and untouchable

We live in a plural democratic society. Democracy is not only a political form of co-existence, but it is a way of thinking, advocated by individuals and society. Democratic thought emphasises individual freedom. The entire society strives to provide as much freedom as possible to each of its citizens. One of the necessary pre-conditions for peaceful co-existence within a plural democratic society is tolerance, i.e. respect for various opinions. Within the democracy, there exist various interpretations as regards morally-admissible actions; in the field of ethics there also exists pluralism of various perceptions. We often disagree on whether a specific action should be regarded as a morally admissible act or not. This is not surprising since there exist various convictions and beliefs about life and the world. Despite all these, we should be aware of the fact that we co-exist and shape our society together, so we have to agree which common values our society will strive for. This ethic minimum or world ethos is one of the preconditions for mutual dialogue. At this point one should enumerate a few basic principles that are founded on the respect for human dignity and that, also, advocate the untouchability of human life. They include the following:

1. All human lives are equally important and they should be treated as such.
2. One should never kill an unborn child.
3. Human life should be perceived as a precious gift.

Due to the topicality of the issues presented, for legislative purposes, as well as due to the necessity for certain important documents advocating the primary and absolute value of human life the Pontificial Council for Pastorale Assistance decided to publish a specific document entitled the "Charter for Health Care Workers".[1] This document provides some important guidelines that health care workers and other experts should respect in their work, since the document

1 Herafter CW.

is based on the principles of general humanity. The Christian morality is also based on those principles. The document could be perceived as a synthesis of the Hippocratic ethics and Christian morality. In its very beginning, the document emphasises the basic characteristics of the deontological for those engaged in health and, also, presents our, Christian attitude to bioethics:

"The work of health care persons is a very valuable <service to life>. It expresses a profoundly human and Christian commitment, undertaken and carried out not only as a technical activity but also as one of dedication to and love of neighbor. It is 'a form of Christian witness.' 'Their profession calls for them to be guardians and servants of human life' (<Evangelium Vitae> 89)." (CH, 1)

Life is a primary and fundamental good of the human person. Caring for life, then, expresses, first and foremost, a truly human activity in defense of physical life. Professional or voluntary health care workers devote their activity right to this – to caring for life. Among them are doctors, nurses, hospital chaplains, administrators, voluntary care givers for those who suffer, those involved in the diagnosis, treatment and recovery of human health. "The principal and symbolic expression of 'taking care' is their <vigilant and caring presence at the sickbed>. It is here that medical and nursing activity expresses its lofty human and Christian value." (CH, 1)

"Health care activity is based on an interpersonal relationship of a special kind. It is 'a meeting between trust and conscience.' /…/ The 'trust' of one who is ill and suffering and hence in need, who entrusts himself to the 'conscience' of another who can help him in his need and who comes to his assistance to care for him and cure him. This is the health care worker. For him 'the sick person is never merely a clinical case'—an anonymous individual on whom to apply the fruit of his knowledge—'but always a 'sick person,' towards whom' he shows a sincere attitude of 'sympathy,' in the ethymological sense of the term.' /…/" (CH, 2)

This requires love: availability, attention, understanding, sharing, benevolence, patience, dialogue. 'Scientific and professional expertise' is not enough; what is required is 'personal empathy with the concrete situations of each patient.' /…/" (CH, 2)

In the field of ethics, there exist two main trends: a) Bioethics which advocates the quality of life (in the negative sense of the word) by implying that scientists can employ all the possible means in their research; individual freedom is the most important value in this case (the main representative of this trend is the Australian philosopher Peter Singer); b) bioethics which advocates the untouchability and the sacredness of life by emphasising that man is neither the sole master of his own life nor can he control the destinies of other people. In the latter case, life is perceived as a gift, as a sacred thing. However, as soon as one accepts life as a gift, one is obliged to take responsibility for his own life, for the lives of other people and for life in general as well. If one considers various dilemmas and extremely rapid advances in health care, there emerges the key issue: Has one's ethical sensibility really developed to such an extent that one will not abuse the power one has acquired due to large technological and scientific development? Can one responsibly employ the advances of our time? Does man really know how to act in a responsible way so that the power he possesses will not eventually turn against him?

Bioethics, research on human beings, and risks of misuse

Recent advances in biology and medicine presuppose a new era in the history of mankind. One cannot really predict the after-effects that could occur due to many findings and new genetic manipulatory interventions, not even for the individual and not for society as well. One will definitely observe certain after-effects of the benefits occurring. This will probably result in a transformed attitude to human dignity, which can, in the long run, also influence one's attitude to human rights and to the well-being of each individual. The dignity and the life of in vitro embryos are definitely threatened by the interests of scientists and commissioners. Certain countries have legitimised the "creation" of human embryos and/or the cloning of human beings, which legitimately objectifies human life. The technology of in vitro fertilisation can now be abused for many new, morally-questionable purposes. Society should constantly monitor scientific experimentation and various applications of the new knowledge to ensure that the appropriate ethical standards are respected in these cases; this necessity has been strongly verified by the past as well as by contemporary clinical experimentation. Monitoring is especially important in this time and era when various interests and expectations, associated with experimentation on human beings, are the greatest ever. Unfortunately, even the so-called practical ethics cannont convince scientists or commissioners to respect the necessary moral standards.

One would not exaggerate if one emphasised that the very advances in biology and medicine marked the beginning of a new era in the history of mankind. However, it is especially hard to predict what after-effects the individual and society could experience due to the new findings from the field of genetics. One should definitely address many new issues associated with human rights and human dignity. But, certain solutions may not be very promising for the future of mankind. If one discusses bioethics, one cannot ignore its history. In the past scientists did not only enter many, unexplored fields, but they also faced enormous risks since they could not predict the after-effects and the dangers of the experiments they engaged in. However, one should emphasise that, in the majority of cases, scientists pursue certain worthy, noble causes. Often the experiments were conducted on the very researchers, which was, by a generally accepted definition, the only ethically admissible type of experimentation on human beings.

However, there also occurred many tragic events, characterised by abuses. One should emphasise that in scientific experimentation there have always appeared abuses, from its very beginning to the new era. The worst of these occurred in the twentieth century when more than ten thousand people suffered, fell seriously ill or even died after engaging in medical research and experimentation on human beings. These people participated in the experiments without any rational explanation and without their informed consent; often, they were not even informed that they were participating in a scientific experiment. One can read many heart-breaking descriptions about this type of experimentation. One would probably associate these with the crimes of German doctors from the Nazi concentration camps. But, these were not the worst possible crimes – during the Second World War even more terrible experiments and, also, sheer savageries (such as vivisection and the anaesthesia-less dissection of half-dead war prisoners of war), were conducted by various Japanese doctors. For the sake of these victims, it would not be fair if one merely presented a brief overview of these inhuman crimes characterised by unimaginable, consciously-caused suffering and pain. However, one must not forget that such, inhuman abuses had also occurred prior to the Second World War and that they continued well after it. There exist many descriptions of several thousand morally reprehensible post-war experiments in the USA (Hassner Sharav, *Human Experiments: A Chronology of Human Research*).

One could enumerate various reasons and motives for these abuses, from ambition, to the desire for a faster promotion and better earnings, and even to inconsideration and the "criminal" ignorance of the very researchers. However, the most terrible ethically reprehensible actions appeared in the 20th century these were committed by scientists who were influenced by certain ideologies, by the requirements of the "criminal" regimes, and also by the economic ambitions of certain influential pharmaceutical companies. In the majority of the cases, the "perpetrators" were renowned doctors and scientists who were perceived as trustworthy experts from the field of medicine and science.

And who were, then, the "victims" of these terrible crimes? These were the most fragile, the least protected as well as the most sensitive members of society, i.e. those suffering from serious diseases, the elderly, the poor, the mentally ill, the orphans, the underprivileged – prisoners, prisoners of war, subordinate employees, soldiers, and unborn babies. These people had to participate in the experiments without any rational explanation or their informed consent; often, they were not even informed that they were participating in a scientific experiment. But, the commissioners and the payers of these morally-questionable and morally-inadmissible experiments were not merely pharmaceutical companies; surprisingly, these were also different governmental organisations. Here one should mention various, renowned American institutions, such as the Ministry of Defence, The Ministry of Energy, U.S. Public Health Service, Atomic Energy Commission, CIA, the U.S. Army, the Environmental Agency, and the U.S. Government. The "perpetrators" even included various national health institutions and large medical centres and universities. Often, the "scientific" part of these "criminal" experiments was not well-conducted, so the findings were useless in many cases. Many of these "studies" were never officially announced as "experimentation"; these were mere, vague ideas of the type "Let us try and see what will happen in the end". Thus, these studies were based on vague ideas and improvised experiments where no safety or security precautions were respected. One can imagine that the public never learned about many of these irresponsible and criminal, pseudo-scientific pilot projects.

The protocol on human genetics is focused on genetic testing for health reasons

The most recent protocol complementing the Convention for the Protection of Human Rights is the Draft Protocol to the Convention for the Protection of Human Rights on Genetic Testing for Health Purposes (2007). This is a carefully prepared legal-ethical document based on widely international unanimity. The protocol in question, which was accepted and published and, later, subjected to the scrutiny of the Steering Committee on Bioethics in the very June of 2007, has determined the standards that the legislator bodies should also observe in the application of genetics for medical purposes.

The fundamental principle is the same as the one from the Convention for the Protection of Human Rights and Dignity. Both documents explicitly prohibit every possible form of discrimination of individuals on the basis of their genetic patrimony. Also, when one applies various genetic principles, one should be aware of the fact that the benefits and the well-being of individuals are far more important than the very interests of society and science. The protocol emphasises that the individual has to be given a precise idea of his illness and the nature of the therapeutic interventions; one should be informed about the possible risks, the problems and the consequences that these procedures could entail if one agreed to or if one refused the therapeutical intervention. Additionally, the protocol also emphasises one's right to the free choice in such interventions. Genetic research which can reveal the existence of a hereditary disease or discover the presence of a gene which can cause a disease or ascertain certain predispositions, can only be employed for health or scientific purposes. The individual who is to be subjected to the treatment, should be informed about the possible consequences the treatment might entail: about the diagnosis and the prognosis for the future, about the possible implications that the results might have for the decisions about one's future children, about the consequences the therapeutic intervention could entail for other family members. The individual should also be informed about various types of help available to him, from genetic counselling to various types of advice and help in the cases of additional therapeutic interventions. The protocol especially mentions the rights of the individuals with a temporary or a permanent loss of knowing and will. Genetic testing has to be postponed in the case of children and adolescences until they have reached their majority, unless such postponement would harm these individuals or threaten their earthly existence.

Confidentiality is another significant issue here. Genetic patrimony is a specific type of confidential information which a person only partially discusses with the other members of his family. Should individuals publicly reveal some delicate information about their genetic patrimony? If an individual decides for this, he could violate his relatives' right for privacy and, thus, he would expose them to stigmatisation and discrimination. Such manipulation should not be prohibited only to doctors but also to individuals who professionally deal with these data.

On the other hand, everybody has the right to be informed about their medical condition. They should also be able to gain access to other information which is not directly associated with their physical health. Health care workers also have to respect the patient's desire in the case when the patient does not want to be informed about certain information.

Thus, the Steering Committee on Bioethics (with the Council of Europe) continues with its patient and precise work, by carefully amending the established ethical standards protecting individual from unjustified medical and biological experimentation. However, one still needs to resolve some rather difficult questions. Genetic technology, which detects certain diseases or ascertains the predispositions for these diseases, also provides some other, ethically more delicate procedures such as gene therapy which tries to modify various genetic anomalies. The protocol mentioned already prohibits such genetic manipulation on clinical cells that would, as a result, enable that the "modified" gene of the patient, altered due to certain congenital genetic anomalies, would be also acquired by the genome of all the patient's own descendants by way of genetic inheritance. In the long run this type of research will not be a safe-enough procedure since there could appear certain, unpredictable after-effects. The protocol also forbids various in vitro techniques enabling the "production" of one's children according to sex or other predetermined qualities; the use of such artificial means is morally-admissible only in the cases where it prevents serious diseases or certain serious malformations of the fetus. Unfortunately, the convention and the protocol have not managed to resolve some other burning issues such as the preconceptual as well as prenatal testing. There also remains the issue of the genotypization of the entire populations that, besides resulting in various beneficial results for humanity, could also be subjected to various grave abuses.

References

Charter for Health Care Workers. Pontifical Council for Pastoral Assistance. Available on-line at: file:///C:/Users/Uporabnik/Documents/Celje%202015/book/Council%20for%20Pastoral%20Assistance%2030%2010%2016.htm#4. (Accessed on October 10, 2016.)

Convention for the Protection of Human Rights and Dignity of the Human Being with Regard to the Application of Biology and Medicine: Convention on Human Rights and Biomedicine. 1997. European Treaty Series - No. 164. Council of Europe (Directorate of Legal Affairs), Oviedo.

Draft Protocol to the Convention for the Protection of Human Rights and Dignity of the Human Being With Regard to the Application of Biology and Medicine, on Genetic Testing for Health Purposes. 2007. CDBI (2004) 14 REV7, Strasbourg.

Hassner Sharav, V. *Human Experiments: A Chronology of Human Research.* Available on-line at: http://www.newpatriotsblog.com/news/human-experiments-a-chronology-of-human-research/. (Accessed on August 13, 2015.)

AM I CHARLIE? RELIGION, TRUTH AND TOLERANCE IN MULTICULTURAL URBAN NEIGHBOURHOODS

Mark Kleyman, Ivanovo

Introduction

The paper aims to examine some socio-cultural and socio-psychological factors that impact on the emergence of multicultural urban communities in Europe. At the same time, it concentrates on discussing the (possible) ways to minimize the negative consequences of these processes. In searching for the ways out of the current situation, the EU's top representatives often put an emphasis on developing policies and practices of multiculturalism across Europe, but the problem is how such policies and practices are often understood and implemented. According to Bojan Žalec (2015a), some forms of multiculturalism should be supported and some rejected. The utilitarian attitude towards multiculturalism inevitably resulted in the point of view, according to which all cultures are intrinsically good. To describe such approach, which is in many respects close to cultural relativism, Bojan Žalec introduces the term "*leveling multiculturalism*" (Žalec 2015a, 53), because, in fact, this approach entails leveling every culture. As the consequence, from the perspective of leveling multiculturalism there is no need to cultivate the distinct European identity, whereas, as Larry Siedentop (2001) argues, the European identity is rooted back to liberal attitudes that, in return, are of Christian origin. The main research question is thus about the ethical principles that could provide a (possible) alternative of leveling multiculturalism.

The paper begins with the analysis of the challenges posed by the series of terrorist attacks and refugee crisis to the stable development of Europe. It continues with the critical evaluation of the different attitudes towards multiculturalism within the EU, with the special emphasis on the "tolerance of the non-tolerant" conundrum. The next part attempts to answer the question why the current situation produces the widespread disbelief in democracy as the best road to the solution of the most haunting social problems. In the concluding part, it is argued that the idea of solidary personalism may underpin universal truth of human dignity being a goal by itself. In return, this idea may be regarded as a background of cultivating tolerance within multicultural urban neighborhoods.

The challenges of diasporization

The year 2015 started with the terrorist attack of political assassins on the highly media-visible French newsmagazine *Charlie Hebdo*. Later on Europe faced with the unprecedented refugee crisis, and the end of 2015 was marked by the multiple terrorist attacks claimed by Islamic State of Iraq and the Levant (ISIL) in Paris on 13th of November, resulting in 130 fatalities. This has produced many pessimistic predictions of Europe's forthcoming apocalypse. Yet, the main question is whether these challenges are distinctly new or they are merely a consequence of the earlier development of the EU.

In fact, for the last decades Europe has experienced massive labor migration and the influx of refugees. According to Zygmunt Bauman (2015), this has resulted in transforming the distant stranger, or briefly visiting stranger, or passing-by stranger, into a next-door neighbor who shares the street, public facilities, workplace and school. In this context, the challenges posed in 2015 are new merely in regards to their scale, whereas they are rooted back to the previous development of Western Europe.

At the same time, the situation is distinctly new for the former Communist countries of Central and Eastern Europe that have been put at the forefront of the current refugee crisis. Thus far, the "new" EU's member states have not been a preferable destination for most of the immigrants (due to the higher standards of social welfare in the "old" EU's countries). Whereas most of the refugees still consider the "new" EU's member states (first of all, Hungary) merely as an entry point into the more affluent Western European countries (such as, for instance, Germany), the post-Communist Europe also begins to face with the diasporization of urban neighborhoods. For instance, more than 1,450 refugees per 100,000 of Hungary's local population claimed asylum in the first half of 2015, to compare with the figure for Germany of 323 and for the UK of 30 applications for every 100,000 residents. Therefore, although Germany has had the most asylum applications in 2015, the surge of people arriving in Hungary meant it had the highest in proportion to its population. In general, Hungary has moved into the second place for asylum applications within the EU, as it had 174,055 applications by the end of October 2015 (BBC 2015).

Though some of the "new" EU's member states, for instance, the Czech Republic, did not yield to European Union pressure to absorb large numbers of refugees and rejected the EU's quotas, the current situation demonstrates that no European country can avoid the diasporization of urban neighborhoods. The main problem is that the stable development of contemporary Europe is in principle impossible without massive immigration. Due to the low birth rates, long-standing communities are disappearing and the social burden on the young is becoming unsustainable. In this context, the fact that in Kos, Lampedusa and on the Hungarian border thousands of asylum seekers plead to be allowed in, can be considered merely as a consequence, among others, of a population disaster and "ageing" of Europe (Kassam *et al.* 2015). These processes increasingly affect all European countries, regardless of their past experience and cultural backgrounds.

Leveling multiculturalism

The EU's top officials often emphasize the need of developing policies and practices of multiculturalism as a way of dealing with the diasporization of urban neighbourhoods. However, this inevitably reveals the question of how such policies and practices are often understood and implemented.

It seems likely that the idea of any culture being intrinsically good is widely accepted by many EU's top officials and politicians. Such understanding of multiculturalism is closer to cultural relativism: any culture and any cultural praxis is claimed to be morally acceptable, if actually cultivated by some social group (Žalec 2015, 55). From this point of view, every culture is similar to the well-known Nozick's tank (Nozick 1974, 42–45). Being a result of the thought experiment, this tank is an experience machine in which individuals can make unrealistic, pleasurable experience. In so doing, they think that all their wishes have been fulfilled and they live the life they desired at most. Such form of multiculturalism can be addressed as leveling multiculturalism (Žalec 2015a, 53), because in reality this entails leveling every culture. In Stanley Fish's sense, leveling multiculturalism can also be defined as a "boutique" multiculturalism, which means a superficial fascination with the Other. (Fish 1999) Indeed, tasting ethnic food or observing weekend festivals may entail nothing but high-profile flirtations with the Other. As Bauman (2015) argues, boutique multiculturalism is exactly what all the global consumerism attributes mean. Purveyors of this superficial brand of multiculturalism appreciate, enjoy, sympathize with, and recognize the legitimacy of cultures other than their own, and, from this point of view, every culture really seems to be intrinsically good. At the same time, Fish suggests that people inevitably stop approving such a superficial approach towards multiculturalism when they start everyday contacts with a next-door stranger, in regards to taking seriously the core values of the culture he or she tolerates (Fish 1999).

According to Bojan Žalec, leveling multiculturalism is inevitably interlinked with nihilism and instrumentalism. Nihilism can be regarded as a condition of culture in which experiential and intellectual horizons everything is leveled. As the consequence, nihilistic subject cannot perceive a particular cultural tradition as more valuable than any other. As nihilism is practically impossible, it inevitably transforms into some kind of instrumentalism (Žalec 2015a, 19-20).

Instrumentalist attitudes presuppose that a particular person (or, in our case, any culture) cannot be a goal, but (at best) merely a means. Consequently, leveling multiculturalism inevitably entails rejecting liberal principles and respect of human dignity, which are crucial elements of the European cultural identity (Siedentop 2001).

As it seems, the current situation provides an empirical evidence to criticize the main premises of leveling multiculturalism. If we suppose that any culture is intrinsically good, the refugees, who flee from the terroristic ISIL and the oppressive regime of Bashar al-Assad in Syria, would choose the neighboring Arab countries as their main destination. Some of these states, such as, for example, the United Arab Emirates and Saudi Arabia, provide high standards of living. For example, according to the annual World Bank's report, in 2014 the gross domestic product per capita was estimated as 24,161.0 USD for Saudi Arabia, 43,962.7 USD for the United Arab Emirates and 96,732.4 USD for Qatar, to compare with 14,028.7 USD for Hungary, 47,821.9 USD for Germany and 51,190.8 USD for Austria (World Bank 2014). The affluent Arab states increasingly attract labor migrants from many countries. Nevertheless, despite distinct cultural (and administrative) barriers, most of the refugees deliberately choose Europe as their main destination. Therefore, we cannot regard the economic reasons as the main factor which boosts the mass influx of refugees to Europe. These refugees are attracted, first of all, by the distinctive traits of the European culture, as in Europe they mostly seek for security and respect of human rights. But, in return, the very idea of the respect of human rights can be regarded as a unique characteristic of the European cultural traditions, which is rooted back to Christianity (Siedentop 2001, 210 -211)

"Tolerance of the non-tolerant" conundrum

The political assassins, who attacked the French newsmagazine *Charlie Hebdo,* proclaimed that they took vengeance on those who published the cartoons of the Prophet Muhammad. Yet, the fact that the caricatures considered as offensive for Muslims were published by this newsmagazine (and earlier by several Danish and Norwegian newspapers) may be regarded as an attempt to protest against leveling multiculturalism, which often resulted in tolerance of the non-tolerant, as well as an attempt to defend the main principles of the European liberalism. The motto of *Je suis Charlie (I am Charlie)* encompassed millions of people across Europe to protest against the massacre of terrorists. These protests reminded us about the necessity to insist that immigration entails accepting the legitimacy of state enforcement (and, in the EU's case, supra-national enforcement) of liberal principles (Herbert 2001, 63; Žalec 2015b).

Nevertheless, this situation inevitably poses the question whether the cartoons of the Prophet Muhammad are really a proper way to protest against "tolerance of the non-tolerant". According to Ayan Hirsi Ali, the vast majority of Muslims are torn between fundamentalists and terrorists on the one hand and the reformers on the other (cited in Ocvirk 2011, 162). The problem is thus if by choosing the way of protest, that is overtly offensive for all Muslims, against the terrorist massacre we inevitably push Islamic communities towards fundamentalists and terrorists. Accepting the publication of such cartoons as a possible way of protest, we inevitably assume that the Islamic culture as such is intrinsically bad. Paradoxically, this position has a similarity with leveling multiculturalism. Both positions may be regarded as the opposite sides of the same coin, as they consider any culture as a homogenous entity (either intrinsically good or intrinsically bad). Both points of view are based on the idea that every person is determined with characteristics which he or she automatically inherits from his or her community (Žalec 2015a, 26). In reality, however, a particular group is not predetermined and unchangeable; instead, it inevitably represents phenomenal forms of human diversity and plurality, which open up different perspectives on the world and which we can freely form and transform as part of our human conditions (Strahovnik 2015, 58; Benhabib 2011, 51–54; Benhabib 1988). As Erich Fromm (1973) argued, in a world in which violence in every form seems to be increasing, every culture can provide a support for human destructiveness while advocating violence against all regarded as "bad" or "wrong". Consequently, Anthony Appiah (2005) argues that any culture as such is neither good nor bad; therefore, in any culture (including the Islamic culture) we must search for the elements which contribute to the autonomy and flourishing of individuals and support them (Žalec 2015a, 64). At the same time, we should oppose the idea that there is no opportunity for a person to choose his or her own way of accepting or rejecting cultural values of his or her mother culture. On the contrary, from the perspective of liberal multiculturalism the personal freedom of choice is of primary importance (Žalec 2015a, 66). In this context, we should, to some extent, tolerate the intolerant, but the limit of this tolerance represents the violation of personal freedom. In such a case, we distinctly need to accept the enforcement of liberal principles.

How to deal with anti-democratic sentiment

The situation in Europe is widely covered by the state-controlled media in Putin's Russia. Based on the main tenets of the official ideology, many journalists and politicians describe the refugee crisis and the terrorist attacks as the evidence of the failure of democracy in Europe. It is stressed that only the authoritarian and totalitarian regimes, which are based on the rigid top-down power hierarchy, can effectively deal with the main problems of the contemporary world. The media aggressively propagate the idea that the only way out of the current situation is to restore the Iron Curtain and to build up an autarchic model of state capitalism behind it.

Alas, the terrorist attack on the Russian airliner en route to Saint Petersburg from Sharm el-Sheikh killing all 217 passengers and 7 crew members on board on 31 October 2015, demonstrated that in the contemporary world anti-democratic sentiment could not guarantee stability and security. Moreover, this may be regarded as an evidence of Russia being an inherent part of Europe. Despite all the attempts to separate Russia from Europe, we currently face with the same challenges. At the same time, a rising tide of anti-democratic sentiment is not merely a Russian problem. Though in contemporary Russia we witness the extreme forms of that, it is rising all around Europe. In this context, we should not reduce the issue of radicalization and terrorism in Europe to the phenomenon of radical Islamist ideology (Bauman 2015). For example, immediately after the terrorist attacks in Norway on 22nd of July 2011, the media affirmed that this was committed by the Islamist fundamentalists, but soon it was discovered that 77 persons, many of whom were under the age of 18, were killed by a 32-years-old Norwegian, who decided that the practices founded in the idea of tolerance and multiculturalism threatened Europe, and the "right" of defending the European culture would justify any means of obtaining it (Kleyman 2012).

At the same time, we should take into consideration some elements of the Russian cultural heritage that could help us in searching for the ways out of the current situation. The Russian culture not only gave way to Stalinism (which is currently advocated by the top officials of Putin's Russia); it also fostered Leo Tolstoy's idea of the non-resistance to evil by force (Tolstoy [1894] 2013). This idea can remind us that democracy should be based on accepting the universal truth of human dignity being a goal by itself. Among other things, this means no to violence in all its forms (Prijatelj 2015, 111). In this context, from the perspective of liberal multiculturalism the freedom of speech (in our case, to publish any caricatures) can be restricted only in the case if someone overtly propagates and defends violence and crimes against humanity (such as, for instance, in the case of a denial of Holocaust and the crimes of Stalinism). At the same time, we should support some ethical foundations that are in favor to replace these forms of protest with those based on respect of personal dignity regardless of person's cultural and/or religious backgrounds. Yet, it is impossible without telling the truth about the elements of any culture that foster any form of violence.

Concluding remarks

In searching for the possibility of dialogue between the persons who shared different cultural traditions, Albert Schweitzer supported the idea that the European identity was liberal and of Christian origin. At the same time, he pointed out that the history of Europe provided many examples of massacre and violence of human rights. Schweitzer believed that ethical values that could underpin the ideal of true civilization had to have their foundation in deep thought and be world- and life-affirming. He therefore embarked on a search for ethical values in the various major religions and worldviews accessible to him. Finally, he decided that the only thing the people around the world are really sure of is that they live and want to go on living (Brabazon 2005). Consequently, the principle of the Reverence for Life (Schweitzer [1933] 2009), which is rooted back not only to Christian humanism, but to non-Western religious thought, in particular, the Jain principle of *ahimsa* (non-violence), may form an ethical background for searching the foundations of universally valid ethics in an increasingly globalized world (Barsam 2008).

The idea of the Reverence for Life is interlinked with the concept of solidary personalism. The term *"solidary personalism"* was firstly introduced by Bojan Žalec (cf. Žalec 2011a). It presupposes that persons are in principle equal regarding their right to cultivate their singularity or individuality. The main aim of a personalist is flourishing of every person. At the same time, the aim of adjective "solidary" is to stress the relational and participatory nature of a person (Žalec 2011b, 105-6). As Bojan Žalec states, persons are essentially relational beings and must be treated in their concrete situation and historical perspective. Solidarity means not just a kind of economic solidarity but mutual participation of persons on their lives including all their aspects. The central moment of such solidarity is intellectual solidarity (cf. Hollenbach 2003), the participation on the experience of the other (Žalec 2011a, 32). Yet – on the other hand - it is crucial that we recognize that there are limits of inter-personal solidarity: "Solidarity – participation in the life of the other – can however be only partial. The belief that we can reach total participation is dangerous and destroys approaching of the other as the other /…/ and provides contexts for instrumentalization and manipulation" (Žalec 2011b, 106). The cases of Central and Eastern/Southeastern European countries under Communism provide a clear evidence of that.

Consequently, solidary personalism provides a background of criticism of leveling multiculturalism based upon the idea that every culture is intrinsically good, as well as upon the ignorance of the historical context and the current situation of the development of a distinct culture. This provides a framework for dialogic universalism (Hollenbach 2003, 152, n. 23). However, such practices should be developed and established merely through the dialogue between all concerned parties, and this may be regarded as a possible way of establishing porous active borders of the European identity (Müller 2014, 44).The concept of porous active borders presupposes that the European identity should be principally open for any cultural experience. However, such cultural experience should be in favor of the European liberal tradition, which is of Christian origins.

References

Appiah, K. A. 2005. *The Ethics of Identity.* Princeton, NJ: Princeton University Press.

Barsam, A. P. 2008. *Reverence for Life: Albert Schweitzer's Great Contribution to Ethical Thought.* New York: Oxford University Press.

Bauman, Z. 2015. *The Charlie Hebdo Attack and What It Reveals about Society.* Available at: http://www.socialeurope.eu/2015/01/charlie-hebdo/ (Accessed on April 20, 2015).

BBC. 2015. *Migrant Crisis: Migration to Europe Explained in Graphics.* Available at: http://www.bbc.com/news/world-europe-34131911 (Accessed on December 24, 2015).

Benhabib, S. 1988. Judgment and the Moral Foundations of Politics in Arendt's Thought. *Political Theory* 16 (1), pp. 29-51.

Benhabib, S. 2011. *Dignity in Adversity. Human Rights in Troubled Times.* Cambridge: Polity.

Brabazon, J. 2005. *Albert Schweitzer, Essential Writings.* New York: Orbis Books.

Fish, S. 1999. *The Trouble with Principle.* Cambridge, MA: Harvard University Press.

Fromm, E. 1973. *The Anatomy of Human Destructiveness.* New York. Henry Holt.

Herbert, D. 2001. Virtue Ethics, Justice and Religion in Multicultural Societies. In: Flanagan, K. and Jupp, P. S. (eds.), *Virtue Ethics and Sociology: Issues of Modernity and Religion.* Basingstoke; New York: Palgrave Macmillan, pp. 51–67.

Hollenbach, D.S.J. 2003. *The Common Good and Christian Ethics.* Cambridge (UK): Cambridge University Press.

Kassam, A., Scammell R., Connolly, K., Orange, R., Willsher, K. and Ratcliff, R. 2015. Europe Needs Many More Babies to Avert a Population Disaster. *The Guardian,* August 23, 2015. Available at: http://www.theguardian.com/world/2015/aug/23/baby-crisis-europe-brink-depopulation-disaster (Accessed on December 24, 2015).

Kleyman, M. 2012. Urban Development, Grassroots Authoritarianism and the Problem of Reconciliation in Post-Soviet Russia. In: Juhant, J. and Žalec, B. (eds.), *Reconciliation: The Way of Healing and Growth.* Berlin: Lit, pp. 241–248.

Müller, K. 2014. European Civil Society Conundrum: Public Sphers, Identities and the Challenge of Politicisation. *Central European Journal of International and Security Studies* 8 (1), pp. 32–55.

Nozick, R. 1974. *Anarchy, State, and Utopia.* New York: Basic Books.

Ocvirk, D.K. 2011. Muhammad: What Kind of Behaviour Pattern? In: Juhant, J. and Žalec, B. (eds.), *Humanity after Selfish Prometheus: Chances of Dialogue and Ethics in a Technicized World.* Berlin: Lit, pp. 159-166.

Prijatelj, E. 2015. Suicide and Genocide from the Perspective of Identities and Narcissism. In: Juhant, J. and Žalec, B. (eds.), *Understanding Genocide and Suicide.* Berlin: Lit, pp. 111–118.

Schweitzer, A. [1933] 2009. *Out of My Life and Thought.* 60th Anniversary Edition. Baltimore, MD: Johns Hopkins University Press.

Siedentop, L. 2001. *Democracy in Europe.* London: Allen Lane.

Strahovnik, V. 2015. On the Concept of Genocide from the Point of View of Groups and Harm. In: Juhant, J. and Žalec, B. (eds.), *Understanding Genocide and Suicide.* Berlin: Lit, pp. 53–60.

Tolstoy, L. [1894] 2013. The Kingdom of God Is Within You. Available at: http://www.gutenberg.org/files/43302/43302-h/43302-h.htm (Accessed on December 30, 2015).

World Bank. 2014. *GDP per Capita (Current US$).* Available at: http://data.worldbank.org/indicator/NY.GDP.PCAP.CD (Accessed on December 26, 2015).

Žalec, B. 2011a. Personalism, Truth and Human Rights. In: Juhant, J. and Žalec, B. (eds.), *Humanity after Selfish Prometheus.* Berlin: Lit, pp. 29–41.

Žalec, B. 2011b. On Not Knowing Who We Are: The Ethical Importance of Transcendent Anthropology. *Synthesis Philosophica* 51: 105–115.

Žalec, B. 2015a. *Genocide, Totalitarianism and Multiculturalism. Perspectives in the Light of Solidary Personalism*. Berlin: Lit.

Žalec, B. 2015b. Factors and Indicators of Genocide. In: Juhant, J. and Žalec, B. (eds.), *Understanding Genocide and Suicide.* Berlin: Lit, pp. 25–35.

TRUTH, HISTORY, INTEGRITY, AND RECONCILIATION

Vojko Strahovnik, Ljubljana

1. Introduction

The article explores the relationship between truth, integrity, and reconciliation. The central focus is on the concept of historical truth, which is closely related to the fact that history as a science essentially appeals to the narrative as a form of historical explanation. As the consequence, historical truth is always conditioned by the narrative, which harbours it. Next, I relate the consequences of this to the notion of the integrity of the community and the role that trustfulness and an attitude towards historical truth play within it. In my previous work (Strahovnik 2011; 2012) I have dealt with the role and the importance of shame in processes of reconciliation. This contribution adds to this by focusing specifically on truth and integrity as elements of the reconciliation process.

One of the hallmarks of modern times is the loss of faith in objective truth on the one hand and the variety of ways and means for truth to be manipulated on the other. Historical truth is no exception in this regard and manipulations with it are especially prominent in totalitarian and post-totalitarian societies (cf. Dežman 2014, 614, 623–5). These tendencies are best expressed in the following observations by George Orwell in his essay on Spanish Civil War written in 1943:

> "Early in life I have noticed that no event is ever correctly reported in a newspaper, but in Spain, for the first time, I saw newspaper reports which did not bear any relation to the facts, not even the relationship which is implied in an ordinary lie. I saw great battles reported where there had been no fighting, and complete silence where hundreds of men had been killed. […] I saw, in fact, history being written not in terms of what happened but of what ought to have happened according to various 'party lines'. […] This kind of thing is frightening to me, because it often gives me the feeling that the very concept of objective truth is fading out of the world. After all, the chances are that those lies, or at any rate similar lies, will pass into history. […] Yet, after all, some kind of history will be written, and after those who actually remember the war are dead, it will be universally accepted. So for all practical purposes the lie will have become truth. […] I am willing to believe that history is for the most part inaccurate and biased, but what is peculiar to our own age is the abandonment of the idea that history could be truthfully written. […] The implied objective of this line of thought is a nightmare world

> in which the Leader, or some ruling clique, controls not only the future but the past. If the Leader says of such and such an event, 'It never happened' — well, it never happened. If he says that two and two are five — well, two and two are five. This prospect frightens me much more than bombs — and after our experiences of the last few years that is not a frivolous statement." (Orwell 1943)

The loss of faith in the core of objective truth of course lessens our relationship to it and our commitment to it, and on the other hand opens the doors wide for various manipulations of the truth.

Truth in politics and in public life has its instrumental value (Gaita 2002, 188), with which one aims to achieve some political impact. But in addition to this, the truth (disregarding the manner of its metaphysical justification) has also a non-instrumental, intrinsic value. Often such an understanding of the truth is what witnesses of important historical events have before their minds, e.g. those who testify about events in totalitarian death camps. From the writings of Primo Levi (1984; cf. Gaita 2002, 189) we can see that at the time of greatest distress, suffering and doubts due to the horrors of fascism and Nazism he resorted to chemistry as a rigours science and as a source of a sense of objective truth, verifiability, and clarity. The truth gets close to its non-instrumental worth also in cases, in which it can enrich the lives of people who care about it. It is not just about the value of truth as truth, otherwise this worth could be met with any set of true beliefs. We should have in mind truth as an ideal and truthfulness as a proper attitude towards this ideal. Intellectuals are especially responsible and committed to the truthfulness as holders of this social role (Gaita 2002, 187–213; Juhant 2014, 187). The loss of the faith in objective truth, especially in relation to historical truth, can have devastating effects for reconciliation processes in a given society – as we will try to demonstrate – since it diminishes integrity of this society or groups within it. But, before we can move to this discussion, we should first investigate some difficulties related to historical truth as intimately related to the narrative (form).

2. On historical truth and narrative

The problem of historical truth is closely related to history and historiography as a science. One of the key questions pertains to the role of the narrative as a form of historical knowledge, instrument of explanation, means of understanding and form of reconstruction of the past (Roberts 2001, 1). Two crucial and interconnected questions arise in relation to this. The first question is whether a historian in scientific (re)construction of the past can already find some traces or elements of the narrative or narrative contours in it as it happened. Is the past as it happened already in the form of the narrative or it merely begets this form with historiographical construction? The second question is, if the past as it happened did not have the narrative form, how can we then know whether a narrative is true or that it corresponds to the past itself. About some unconnected heap of past events it is possible to formulate several competing narratives, which cannot all be true and there is no clear set of criteria how to evaluate them in relation to the truth.

Hayden White claims that narratives are "verbal fictions, the contents of which are as much invented as found and the forms of which have more in common with their counterparts in literature than they have with those in the sciences" (White 2001a, 222), thus not found in the past itself. A historical narrative is a narrative interpretation, whose truth should be judged in a different way from a simple form of correspondence of facts with reality. There is thus a sort of narrative theory of truth in play, where simple correspondence is not satisfactory, and where there are several other possible criteria, e.g. coherence, suitableness, adequacy, metaphorical fittingness, etc. A narrative created by a historian is always a sort of construction, based on historical facts and events as key constituents, but its meaning greatly surpasses that of a mere set of atomic facts and events it includes. A historian is faced with an elementary set of events, which have their descriptions and can be spatially and temporally determined, but they nonetheless do not carry with them the part of the meaning they obtain, when they are placed in a certain role in the narrative. Different narratives can convey different meanings to the same events. "Since no given set or sequence or real events is intrinsically 'tragic', 'comic', or 'farcical', but can be constructed as such only by the imposition of the structure of a given story-type on the events, it is the choice of the story-type and its imposition upon the events which endow them with meaning" (White 1984, 20). A key part of the work of the historian is thus not a mere description of events, but interpretation, selection, determination of importance, generalisation, comparison etc.

The problem of the narrative in history is thus closely related to the question of historical truth. On the one hand, we have a view claiming that in order for the historical narrative to be true it should be an exact reconstruction of the past as it happened, if this should then obtain a status of historical knowledge. On the other extreme is a view that all historical narratives, "all stories are allowed, except for the boring ones" (Grdina 1989, 456). One should most probably include all incoherent and nonsensical ones, but as for the rest, which can satisfy the (minimal) criteria of coherence, adequacy, etc. are all acceptable. Factual part of the historical narrative should of course not to be compromised, i.e. fact about past events should not be falsified, although problems emerge also on this level, e.g. due to the lack of historical sources, competing sources or simply because distinct facts do not tell us a lot about the past. It is therefore best to find some middle ground between factual and interpretative elements as regards the truth of the historical narrative.

A Polish historian Jerzy Topolski (1991, 1999) has developed a comprehensive view regarding the criteria or principles for the attribution of truth to a sequence of sentences, stories or narratives as a whole that is situated in this middle ground between factual and interpretative aspects of historical narrative. Irrespective of whether the historian constructs and invents narratives about the past or merely reconstructs them, it aims to the scientific reconstruction of the past and the creation of knowledge. Topolski appeals to a vertical structure of historical narrative, comprising of three substructures:

1. "substructure of information, conveying the narrative wholes constructed by the historian (images of the past);
2. substructure of rhetoric, including all the instruments of persuasion used to address various groups of recipients and to convey to them the meaning of substructure (1);
3. (deep) substructure of politics, which may be called theoretico-ideological, influencing the content of substructure (1) and the rhetoric of substructure (2)" (Topolski 1999, 202).

In historiography, most discussions focus on the issue whether the classical correspondence theory of truth prevails for the historical narrative. A related question is the question of the conditions and rules of the truth of sentences and narratives or stories as a whole. Topolski claims that the latter question is much more significant than the first (1981, 47–48). Historical narrative can be defined as a sequence of non-fictional statements, connected by a common content that relates to the past. Such narratives can be further combined together. As the consequence, the meaning of the entire narrative depends on sub-narratives and statements of which it is composed. Each single part, however, considered separate from the other, thereby loses part of its meaning or its meaning gets deformed. Historical narrative consists mostly of historical statements, while the rest are explanatory or theoretical. A narrative is not a simple conjunction of statements. If this was the case, then one could conclude that the narrative is true if and only if all statements in it are true; and false if at least one statement was false. This is untenable, thus, considering historical narratives we can accept instead the following set of claims: "(1) the truth of all the component statements of an historical narrative (story) does not guarantee the truth of the whole; (2) an historical narrative (story) may remain true even of some of its component statements are false; (3) a proportionately greater share in a narrative (story) of true statements as compared with another narrative (story) does not guarantee a greater degree of truth of the former" (Topolski 1981, 51). One of the consequences of this is that the truth of narratives cannot be evaluated in terms of strict truth conditions and scientific validity. Several narratives about the same historical events can be true (valid, acceptable), yet we take some to be closer to the truth as the others. This is possible if we evaluate them as a whole and if we distinguish between the mentioned sub-structures and their respective functions. With Topolski we must thus conclude that one should not look for some definite criteria for the truth of the narrative on the first (and possibly even including second) level, but merely in the narrative as a whole. The narrative as a whole is composed of several parts: its elements, structure, rules of its structure and coherence. It has a persuasive and explanatory function embedded in the rhetorical level. Given this it can be seen as a persuasive structure; a medium that transmits historian's understanding of the past, the content of his mind and his intentions to the reader that attempts to properly understand or accept it. Imagination and not merely logic is the one that creates more or less concrete mental images of the past within our understanding. In many ways, therefore, the theoretical-ideological level is crucial for a historical narrative as a whole, but at the same time also very elusive and difficult to deal with from a theoretical perspective.

The complexity of the structure of historical narratives also discloses to us that speaking about falsification and unjustified revisions of history (as e.g. prominent in Slovenia), which remains only at a general level, is deeply misguided. The objections would be justified and reasonable if pertaining only to factual level, to the extent that it would reveal false historical statements. At the level of the narrative as a whole, we need to switch to different criteria and a plurality of views (in terms of both, "winners" and "losers") on history. History can thus never be completely ideology-free or neutral historical truth, because as we have seen, as a narrative it is necessarily coupled with the interpretation and evaluation. One aspect of monistic views on historical truth is often the denial or minimization of the victims and "their side of the story" and this proves an especially tough obstacle in the process of reconciliation. Such a waiver or a gap diminishes the integrity of the community, to which we turn now.

3. Truth, identity, integrity and reconciliation

In its primary meaning integrity (from lat. *integer*) means wholeness, completeness, comprehensiveness, coherence and unity, and also a sort of purity. It is closely connected with a healthy moral character, uprightness, honesty and truthfulness. Integrity is not necessarily a characteristic of individuals, but also of institutions, communities or society as a whole. The society with integrity can be understood as a community in which free individuals are recognized as equal, with full human status and dignity and associated with feelings of interdependence, concern for other and affiliation. Such kind of integrity is closely linked to dimensions of responsibility and identity.

A truthful response to our past, to our own history is one precondition of such responsibility. Furthermore, it establishes the identity of the community. "Since we are all caught up in the historical process in which the identity plays an important role, the so-called macro or objective (systemic) factors, such as history or other cultural deposits of groups, nations or global society are important creators of identity and they impact on statehood, geopolitical situation and the development of political institutions and as a result of this also impact wellbeing of its citizens." (Juhant and Strahovnik 2011, 503)

The destruction or falsification of the history of certain groups of people is a crime against them, and such lies could undermine the integrity of the nation or selected community. In other words, the above means that the value of truth can never be reduced only to its use or value for us. "Lies can destroy the integrity of the national life only because we value truthfulness in ways not reducible to the practical benefits it may bring. People find it terrible to live a national lie just as they do to live a lie in their personal lives. In neither case is truthfulness merely a means to something whose value we could understand without appreciating the need we have of truth, for its own sake, as we sometimes say" (Gaita 2002, 188–189).

An important aspect of the integrity of a community or a nation is also that the full recognition of historical truth (including by allowing plurality of reasonable views) refers us to the victims, to those who have been harmed or wronged, and requires reparation of the wrongs done on the one hand; and on the other historical truth can help us understand our relationship to what has been done or what has happened. This can be understood within the context of ethics understood as a way of seeing (Žalec 2014, 212) and in which an important part of this vision is our humble attention to victims.

This is an area of shame and other appropriate moral reactive attitudes (related to identity and integrity), which can reveal to us this relationship and establish or rebuild our personality or our moral identity, both at the individual and community level (Strahovnik 2011). Shame as a response presupposes epistemic (commitment to truth) and the moral dimension (understanding and recognition of responsibility), and at the same time "can motive us to try to reconnect, to work for forgiveness and reconciliation" (Haggerty 2009, 304), but at the level of individual and communities alike. In some cases, an attitude of (restorative) cultivation of shame rather than retributive guilt and retaliation is more productive for reconciliation (Drumbl 2005). All this presupposes a recognition that it is our history, a history of a particular community, and we cannot progress regarding the reconciliation process until such recognition is not present. Reconciliation presupposes recognition of such truth, and so does the assumption of at least part of the responsibility. "When our shame is a lucid expression of collective national responsibility for the wrongs done by our ancestors, we have risen in truthful response to the evil in our history – of the fact that it is our history. Because it is an acknowledgement of the fact that we must rise in truthful moral responsiveness to the meaning of what we have been caught up in, often through no fault of our own, it is rightly called and acceptance of responsibility." (Gaita 2002, 102) Truthfulness is thus a precondition of establishing moral shame, and thus a prerequisite of justice. Žalec also highlights the following important connections between reconciliation and justice: "Reconciliation approach consists of the adoption of restorative, compensatory and (other) requirements of justice, including the future justice. Thus justice is an essential part of the reconciliation process. On the other hand, reconciliation is a positive factor, a basis or even a condition of (future) justice" (Žalec 2013, 167).

It is thus truthfulness that allows us to establish an appropriate response to past events and with this reconciliation. It enables us to avoid such practices of political, judicial or other state institutions in the future that could encourage or set an example to members of the community to foster such indifference towards suffering of those who are victimized, excluded or marginalized. On the contrary, we should promote the full recognition of the humanity of others and our responsiveness to them as our equals. Without such a full attention to the victims there cannot be real justice. A genuine correction of injustices is possible within such horizon.

4. Conclusion

Truthfulness in relation to the historical truth therefore encompasses a recognition of plurality of views and a special attention to all victims. This means overcoming the perspective of history as an exclusive dominance of the winners. Reconciliation process in post-conflict societies is an especially challenging task. In relation to the historical truth one conclusion is that even though different or opposite sides in the reconciliation processes can have compatible or overlapping historical narratives (within the above described perspective of pluralism), they are usually not perceived as such, but as exclusive and non-compatible. One part of the task in reconciliation process is bringing these seemingly exclusive narratives closer together, by giving a special voice to all the victims, which can represent a common ground. This can also be a form of compassion towards them.

References

Dežman, J. 2014. Preseganje travmatskih bremen titoizma [Overcoming Traumatizations Caused by Titoism]. *Bogoslovni vestnik* 74(4): 611–638.

Drumbl, A. M. 2005. Punishment, Postgenocide: From Guilt to Shame to Civis in Rwanda. *New York Law Review* 75: 1221–1326.

Gaita, R. 2002. *A Common Humanity. Thinking about Love and Truth and Justice.* London & New York: Routledge.

Grdina, I. 1989. *Vreme katedrala*, Georges Duby [The Age of Cathedrals – George Duby]. *Zgodovinski časopis*, 43:455–456.

– – –. 2003. *Poti v zgodovino: tri razprave [Pathways into History: Three Essays].* Šentjur: I. Grdina.

Haggerty, D. 2009. White Shame: Responsibiltiy and Moral Emotions. *Philosophy Today*, 53: 304–316.

Juhant, J. 2014. Nasilje in sočutje v ideologijah in religijah in slovenska tranzicijska resničnost [Violence and Compassion in Ideologies and Religions in relation to Slovene Transitional Reality]. *Bogoslovni vestnik* 74, št.2:175–189.

Juhant, J. & Strahovnik, V. 2011. Ali je možna empatična družba dialoga? [Is an empathic society of dialogue possible?]. *Bogoslovni vestnik* 71(4): 495–509.

Levi, P. 1984. *The Periodic Table.* New York: Schocken Books.

Orwell, G. 1943. *Looking back on the Spanish War.* Http://orwell.ru/library/essays/Spanish_War/english/esw_1 (accessed April 10, 2015).

Roberts, G. (ed.) 2001. *The History and Narrative Reader.* New York: Routledge.

Strahovnik, V. 2011. Občutje krivde in sramu v kontekstu sprave. In: Juhant, J., Strahovnik, V. & Žalec, B. (eds) *Izvor odpuščanja in sprave: človek ali Bog: spravni procesi in Slovenci*, Ljubljana: TEOF and Družina, pp. 111–126.

– – –. 2012. Guilt, shame and reconciliation within the context of humanity. In: Janez Juhant in Bojan Zalec, (eds), *Reconcillation. the way of healing and growth*, Münster: Lit Verlag, pp. 129–137.

Topolski, J. 1991. Towards an Integrated Model of Historical Explanation. *History and Theory*, 30(3): 324–338.

– – –. 1999. The Role of Logic and Aesthetics in Constructing Narrative Wholes in Historiography. *History and Theory* 38(2): 198–210.

White, H. 1984. The Question of Narrative in Contemporary Historical Theory. *History and Theory* 23(1): 1–33.

– – –. 2001a. The Historical Text as Literary Artifact. In: Geoffrey Roberts, (ed.), *The History and Narrative Reader*, New York: Routledge, pp. 221–236.

Žalec, B. 2013. Sprava kot način trajnega reševanja konfliktov in njena povezanost s pravičnostjo, z odpuščanjem ter z dialogom [Reconciliation as a way of permanent resolving of conflicts and its connectedness with justice, forgiveness and dialogue]. *Dignitas* 59/60: 203–217.

– – –. 2014. Ljubezen kot enost mnogoterega: kierkegaardovski pogled [Love as unity of variety: a Kierkegaardian view]. *Bogoslovni vestnik* 74(2): 201–213.

LIVING IN A LIE

Jože Dežman, Kranj

> *"Any debate about the civil war is therefore superfluous, because the system was prepared to intervene after the War against any political opponent as an enemy of the people; it was just a matter of whether the civil war would continue in the post-War period." (Vodušek Starič 1992, 38)*

Communists called mass extrajudicial killings "cleansing". Edvard Kardelj (Vice-President of the Yugoslav government) sent the following message to Boris Kidrič (President of the Slovenian government) on 25th of June 1945: "No later than in three weeks, the courts of national honour will be disbanded, military courts will have jurisdiction only over the military, all others will be taken over by ordinary courts. The new amnesty will be proclaimed. You have, therefore, no reason to be as slow with cleansing as before".

Already during the Second World War (8th April 1941–15th May 1945), the communist partisan movement murdered more than 8,000 inhabitants of Slovenia. After the end of the War (mainly in May and June 1945), more than 15,000 inhabitants of Slovenia and probably around 80,000 civilians and prisoners of war of other nationalities were extrajudicially killed by victorious Titoist forces who seized power in Yugoslavia.

The second wave of Titoist "cleansing" was destroying graves. Lawyer Zoran Polič, Minister of the Interior – part of the communist National Government of Slovenia – on 12th June 1945, directed all District National Liberation Committees (NOO): "Therefore the Federal Ministry of the Interior issues on 18. V. 1945 the instruction which requires NOO to take all necessary steps to immediately remove (level to the ground) all cemeteries and individual graves of occupiers and domestic traitors and delete all traces of them." With this command, firstly all graves of murdered persons during the war and post-war murdered inhabitants of Slovenia and Yugoslavia were erased. Some cemeteries where the fallen soldiers of occupying units were buried during the War remained.

The third phase was "cleansing" of collective memory. The system of maintaining and developing revolutionary traditions was an ideological mechanism that, with the help of cult forms and taboos, concealed the crimes and failures of the Yugoslav Communist Party/the League of Communists of Slovenia/Yugoslavia. The purpose of the tabooisation of the crimes of Titoism was to conceal them.

On the basis of all these "cleansings", ideological and racist division of the society was created, Titoist apartheid. As well as the dead, the living were divided. Out of nearly 100,000 casualties of the War, civil war and revolutionary terror between 1941 and 1946, more than 40,000 of the dead were tabooed. The partisan survivors and the relatives of the *holy* dead were given commemorations and rents. The surviving partisan opponents and the relatives and children of the despised dead were forced to remain silent, were denigrated and without recourse to law. The Titoist murders were followed by confiscations and additional taxation; the relatives of the murdered were physically and psychologically tortured and treated as second-class citizens. The raciast discrimination, segregation and stigmatisation affected especially the children of the murdered all the way until the dissolution of Titoism; to this day, the consequences burden many of the survivors. Suffering poverty, beatings and denigration, they were not given help in school, scholarships, many were not allowed access to education; they were usually given bad jobs with no chance of promotion. Because they were not allowed to mourn and most do not know where their close relatives lie buried, many suffer from grief disorders.

Titoists invested extraordinary efforts and significant resources into the tabooization of their crimes. Both political and normal police monitored the relatives of victims and supervised concealed killing grounds and burial places all the way until the end of the Titoist regime in 1990. The importing of emigrant literature in which they wrote about the crimes of Titoism was prohibited in Yugoslavia (Dežman 2008a; 2008b; 2011; 2012).

Declared dead in the Archives of the Commission for the implementation of Redressing of Injustices Act

Applications in the Archives of the Government Commission for the Implementation of Redressing of Injustices Act (below: Commission) also show how both civil servants and relatives of the victims had to avoid the truth about the crime in the official proceedings. All had to "live in a lie".

I have analysed 1503 cases from the Archives of the Commission about how the tabooed victims were declared dead in courts between 1945 and 1990, with 1691 people declared dead, as they would declare up to five murdered people at once (first version of the database was presented in Dežman 2015, 216–219). Likely, there were actually several thousands of such cases. However, the relatives of the murdered victims had to lie in these court proceedings; they had to conceal from the government what they actually knew about the fates of their loved ones. Thousands of judges and other regime members who knew the truth were also forced to lie. This was part of living in a lie in Titoism. Below we present a few examples of how the murdered persons were declared dead, which illustrate how the truth was repressed. At the same time, we recognize how the regime change, democratization and independence of Slovenia (1991) allowed people to tell their truth. According to the new Law on Registers in the years 1995–2009, 4,600 tabooed death victims were declared dead (Predlog Zakona ..., 2010).

Table 1: Number of the tabooed murdered, who were declared dead in the courts in the years 1945–1990 from the Archives of the Commission

When victims were declared dead	Number of cases	Number of victims declared dead
1946–1950	205	224
1951–1960	573	661
1961–1970	378	391
1971–1980	247	285
1981–1990	92	121
unknown year	8	9
Total	1503	1691

Florijan Kopač

Frančiška Kopač, b. on 30th September 1922, submitted a request for the "amnesty for her husband" to the District Court Škofja Loka. Florijan Kopač, b. on 30th March 1917, was a homeguard (domobranci – Slovenian anti-communist units that fought against communist partisans in collaboration with German occupiers – note JD), who retreated with the other homeguards in May 1945 to Carinthia in Austria. From there they were sent back to Slovenia. He was probably murdered in Kočevski Rog in June 1945.

The authorities certainly knew that he was murdered, yet the District Court Škofja Loka on 21st December 1945 wrote to Frančiška Kopač: "The court informs you that your request for clemency was delegated to the Military Court of the military district Ljubljana as the relevant authority. Death to Fascism - Freedom to the people!"

On 25th December 1945, the Military Court remitted the application of Kopač to District Court: "We return the request because Kopač Florijan was not tried in our court." This statement confirms that Kopač and more than 15,000 killed in May and June 1945 were killed extrajudicially.

Florijan Kopač was declared dead at the District Court in Kranj on 30th April 1948. On 22nd April 1998, Frančiška Kopač stated in her application to the Commission: "I was a young widow without any income with two young children (first son was born on 19th March 1943, the second on 21st July 1945). It was difficult to live without anything and without any support. We were all neglected and despised and mocked. The kids did not even know their father. For all I am left alone. Even today we are all despised and we still live in fear" (Archive, file 71401-1604-98).

Janez Pestotnik

The District Court in Kamnik declared Janez Pestotnik dead on 29th September 1953 – five years after they found his remains.

Pestotnik's daughter wrote in a statement to the Commission on 31st March 2003:

"My father, Janez Pestotnik, was the courier of the Commander of the (partisan – note JD) Kamnik Detachment. In December 1944, the detachment completely disintegrated. The soldiers were instructed to save themselves in any way they could. …. He went home to his family in Mali Jelnik and shortly thereafter reported at the German Gendarmerie in Blagovica.

In Blagovica, he remained until liberation in May 1945. After the liberation, the father got a message from a former commander of the detachment whose courier he was during the war via his brother and brother-in-law, to report at the municipality in Blagovica.

My father and his brother did so. They went to the municipality in Blagovica, from where they did not come back and nobody saw them since then.

Three years later, in December 1948, a neighbour – peasant woman – at work in the woods near Blagovica found human bones. The grave was excavated and in it, they found the remains of two adult men. Using the apparel, shoes and teeth, they identified my father and uncle. My father with a broken skull, uncle with a gunshot hole in the skull. I think that this is sufficient proof that my father died after the liberation of violent death.

The hardships of suffering and interrogations of my family experienced during the years 1945–1948 and later I will deliberately not describe" (Archive, file 714-01-176-2003).

Mihael Štravs

The decision of the District Court of Novo mesto from 17th September 1956 by which Michael Štravs was declared dead, states:

"Missing Štravs Mihael had gone with homeguards after the liberation to Koroška (Carinthia in Austria – note JD), because he was mobilized by the Germans and the homeguards, he was returned from Carinthia in the country and in

August ended up in a camp in Teharje and there has been no news about him and he has not sent a word home since then.

The District People's Committee, the Secretariat for Internal Affairs, in Novo Mesto announced that there is no information about the missing Štravs Mihael since 1945, that the authorities have not been able to establish that the missing was on the territory of the FLRJ (Federativna ljudska republika Jugoslavija – Federal People's Republic of Yugoslavia), nor that the missing resides inside or outside of the territory of the FLRJ.

The public announcement, which was published in the Official Journal of FLRJ on 13. 6. 1959 under Art. 25 was not answered."

In the application for reparation of injustices on 8th April 1998, Mihael's brother Štefan Štravs indicated, that in the communist extermination camp Teharje he saw how his brother was taken to his death: "I was present when my brother Miha was loaded in a truck in Teharje with other prisoners. It was the first transport."(Archive, file 71401-1174-98)

Rudolf Herman

Rudolf Herman, b. on 16th September 1900, was mobilized by the partisans in 1944, and he was soon discharged because of poor hearing. As a farmer, he then supported the partisans with material goods. On 12th June 1945, four members of the new authorities conducted an investigation in his home. They were looking for material to be acquired after the capitulation of Germany. Herman was taken to the nearby farm, where he was imprisoned in the cellar and beaten to death with sticks.

The District Public Prosecutor's Office in Celje only on 17th June 1947, filed an indictment against Ivan Zupanc (1907), Jože Hrvatin (1921), Anton Žagar (1926) and Albin Privšek (1928) for offense against life and limb. The trial was scheduled for 8th July 1947, but the Criminal Division of the District Public Prosecutor's Office in Celje on 2nd July 1947 withdrew the indictment. Herman was not pronounced dead until the judgment of the District Court in Celje on 17th October 1949 (Archive, file 714-01-921-2001; Dežman 2015, 80–81).

Action in the night from 26th to 27th March 1948

The political police inserted covert agents into the anti-communist group, which operated in Slovenske gorice along the border with Austria. The group did not carry out any actions, especially not armed. Directed by the political police, the members of the group gathered at the home of Rupert Hüttler in Selnica ob Muri. In the attack in the night from 26th to 27th March 1948, probably 14 members of the group were killed, another one was later sentenced to death and executed. Rupert Hüttler fled to Austria.

The deaths of some of the killed were recorded in the death registers. E.g. for Franc Hüttler the date of death is inscribed as "27th (twenty-seventh) March 1948 at 2:00 pm".

Štefanija Roškar, the wife of killed Franc Roškar submitted the "Report of death" four months after the event, on 20th July 1948. The application of death stated that he died on 27th March 1948, at three in the morning in Selnica ob Muri and that he "burnt with the house - corpse was not found".

On 3rd May 2005, a witness confessed that he went to "the place of the event together with his half-brother and neighbours. When they came to the homestead, there were stopped by Udba (political police – note JD) guards in civilian clothes. Because they did not let them in, they have returned there on Easter Sunday. Bodies were still present (around 12). Some corpses lay in the house and the outbuilding, but some of them lay down a hill. The bodies that were on the hill were recognizable as they were apparently shot, whereas some of the bodies in the house were unrecognizable because of the fire. Roškar Franc was lying in the house and next to him was Dajčman Erhard. Roškar Franc was partially burned, he was identified by the wallet he had with him".

So, we can conclude that the authorities took the remains of the killed to an unknown location.

Erhard Dajčman, b. on 9th December 1911, from Somati was also killed. He was declared dead by the decision of the District Court in Maribor - Surroundings dated 20th March 1951. The next day after the fire, three witnesses were ordered to "clean up the place where the house burned down last night." In doing so, they were instructed that all papers and documents and other items that would be found among the rubble, should be carefully collected and given to the Department of the Interior. Two witnesses found Dajčman's wallet (documents, pictures of wife and children).

In her application to the Commission on January 2002, Dajčman's daughter (b. 1942) indicated the mistreatment of the government against children: "I am not able to get any information, because I'm still the bandit's daughter; because it is not available online, I cannot get it for you. Please, if you can investigate why the secret police killed my father, why they put a machine gun to my head and tried to kill me. Tell me, where the grave of my father is, so that I may light a candle for him. They killed him without trial." The other daughter (b. 1940) states that "she had problems with employment, enrollment in school, and that is also why she was not accepted anywhere" (Archive, file 714-01-841-2003; Dežman 2015, 205–2008).

Ivan Mencinger

Ivan Mencinger was arrested in Celje on 21st June 1945. The record of the interrogation on 23rd June 1945, is preserved: "I deny and protest my denunciation and I beg to be interrogated in front of the accuser. I received a Cross of Merit for lengthy and diligent service, because I have been with the firm 18 years, always good and conscientious worker." Postscript under the record of the interrogation ("03.08.45 2.20") may indicate the date and time when Mencinger was taken to his death. It was on the day of the amnesty.

Hoping that Mencinger was still alive and that he would possibly return, his wife kept looking for him until 1950 at various camps and authorities in charge for Styria, but in vain. Therefore, in the summer of 1950, she submitted an application to the District court in Celje to declare Ivan Mencinger dead.

The District Court on 5th June 1950, ruled that Mencinger on the basis of unsuccessful inquiries was no longer alive since 1st January 1946: "Mencinger Ivan was arrested by our authorities on 21st July (correct date is 21st June - JD) and brought to prison, after that no trace could be found."

This decision enabled his wife to submit a request for granting a pension, application is dated 9th June 1950. Before that, she was completely dependent on monetary support from relatives. She started receiving pension in January 1951. Before she got the pension, a reference of Ivan Mencinger was written by the Secretariat of the Communist Party Gaberje on 11th October 1950. It disproved the charges for which Mencinger was murdered: "The named has not been sentenced either to the loss of national honour or to the loss of civic honour, or the loss of honorary rights. He did not lose either political or individual civil rights. During the occupation, he was not under arms of the occupier nor his helpers. He was not organized or active member of quisling organizations and he was not suspected of such work. He has moved away from our area in 1945 and from that time onwards his life is not known to us."

After the first democratic elections in the Socialist Republic of Slovenia, the relatives of the murdered were trying to find more information. Mencinger's daughter wrote on 6th June 1990, to the Council for the Protection of Human Rights: "They never told us what they did with him. Maybe the time has come when anything could be found out about it?"

The Council wrote to the Secretariat of the Interior of Socialist Republic of Slovenia, and from there on 9th July 1990 came a negative answer: "We are sorry, but we cannot do anything. However, we cannot say that the case is hopeless, because eventually some new records may appear where a trace might be found. Therefore, we recommend that in time you contact the Republican Secretariat of the Interior directly."

Mencinger's son and daughter described the family tragedy in the letter to the Commission on 1st December 2004: "This tragic event completely destroyed our family. Without a father, a husband to support us, we immediately had to move from the factory apartment. We remained without rights and financial resources. With great difficulty, father's relatives found us a very modest apartment in Jesenice. They helped us with cash contributions since we were without anything."

Just like many other relatives, Janja and Marjan wish to bury their father: "The individual articles of the law Redress of Injustices Act lead to our rights; but we would especially like to find out what has actually happened with our father respectively, to set up his final resting place, if possible" (Archive, file 714-01-1020-2004)

No longer living in a lie

The daughter and son of Ivan Mencinger were my neighbours in Lesce. But, until I read their file in the archives of the Commission, I did not know that their father was murdered. But, with thousands of such testimonies, the Titoist taboo is falling apart.

It reveals that the authorities kept records all the way until the collapse of the regime, where the murdered were listed, as well as supervising the concealed killing and burial sites. Doris Pahor in her case study discovered that the political police stored data about people who were murdered by the partisan movement during the War and by the communist authorities after the War all the way until the collapse of the regime (1991).

In CAE (Centralna aktivna evidenca - Centrale active record) Pahor found 27 out of 88 victims that were murdered in Carst abyss Pri Konfinu I. From 217 persons murdered on the command of Mitja Ribičič the result of the survey of the CAE is (Pahor 2011):

The identity of enrollment in CAE is confirmed	151 (69.6 %)
No enrollment in CAE	47 (21.7 %)
It is not possible to confirm or reject the enrollment in CAE	19 (8.7 %)

We can say that the breakdown of Titoist taboos is also a fundamental transitional process in Slovenia. The victims of Titoism are a proof of Solzhenitsyn's words: "Either truth or falsehood: Toward spiritual independence or toward spiritual servitude" (Solzhenizsyn 1974). The complicated process is far from completion.

References

Archive of the Government Commission for the Implementation of Redressing of Injustices Act.

Dežman, J. 2008a. Communist repression and transitional justice in Slovenia. In: P. Jambrek (ed.), *Crimes committed by totalitarian regimes: reports and proceedings of the 8th April European Public Hearing on Crimes Committed by Totalitarian Regimes*. Ljubljana: Slovenian Presidency of the Council of the European Union, pp. 197–206.

Dežman, J. 2008b. Tranzicijska pravičnost. In: J. Dežman (ed.), *Poročilo Komisije Vlade Republike Slovenije za reševanje vprašanj prikritih grobišč: 2005-2008*. Ljubljana: Družina, pp. 251–431.

Dežman, J. 2011. Tabuizacija in detabuizacija. In: J. Dežman (ed.), *Resnica in sočutje: prispevki k črni knjigi titoizma: poročilo 3: poročilo Komisije Vlade RS za reševanje vprašanj prikritih grobišč 2009-2011*. Ljubljana: Družina, pp. 131–248.

Dežman, J. 2012. Slovenia and the criminal burden of Titoism. In: J. Juhant and B. Žalec (eds), *Reconciliation: the way of healing and growth*. Zürich; Münster: Lit Verlag, pp. 221–231.

Dežman, J. 2015. *Ni bilo lahko – a smo stali in obstali*. Celovec: Mohorjeva založba, pp. 216-219.

Pahor, D. 2011. Ali je tajna služba še po vojni za obrambo Republike Slovenije razpolagala s podatki o žrtvah zunajsodnih pobojev? In: J. Dežman (ed.), *Resnica in sočutje: prispevki k črni knjigi titoizma: poročilo 3: poročilo Komisije Vlade RS za reševanje vprašanj prikritih grobišč 2009–2011*. Ljubljana: Družina, pp. 121–130.

Predlog Zakona o spremembah in dopolnitvah zakona o matičnem registru. 2010. Http://vrs-3.vlada.si/imis/imisnet.nsf/0/7653E17152AE-7285C1257F30002A4DF0/$FILE/t8346535.PDF?OpenElement (accessed on December 13, 2015).

Solzhenitsyn, A. 1974. Live Not by Lies. http://www.orthodoxytoday.org/articles/SolhenitsynLies.php (accessed on December 28, 2015).

Vodušek Starič, J. 1992. *Prevzem oblasti 1944-1946*. Ljubljana: Cankarjeva založba.

SYMPATHY WITH OTHER'S PRIDE - AN ADDITION FOR THE POLITICS OF RECOGNITION

Béla Mester, Budapest

A characteristic feature of the classical model of toleration, rooted in the ideas of the political philosophy of the early modernity is a privileged epistemological position of the person who formulates the ideas and rules of the tolerant behaviours, and opinions. It is inevitable that it emerges as a point of view of an *omniscient spectator* whose position is *above all* the interests, prides, faiths, superstitions and customs of the people, in this system of toleration. In a recent writing of mine published in the previous volume of the same series of books I have analysed the structure of the key text of this discourse, Locke's *Letter Concerning Toleration* from the point of view of the position of the author as an uninterested spectator (Mester 2016). In a few of my recent writings, I have analysed several features of the classical religious toleration from the point of view of the *pictorial philosophy* (e.g. Mester 2014). In a recent paper, I have analysed the historical narrative of *religio duplex* formulated by Jan Assmann, in his last monograph as a basis of the religious toleration of the Enlightenment (Mester 2015; Assmann 2010).

All of my investigations have concluded to the same result about the structure of the classical model of toleration; within the framework of this concept we can tolerate things and phenomena, which are meaningless and valueless for ourselves, regardless to the value and meaning which appears for the people whose behaviour and opinions we tolerate. This kind of toleration must neglect the *identity* of the people, and communities, who are tolerated by us, and disregards their *pride* as an emotional element of their identities. Something that must be tolerated by us can be a part of the *pride* of other people. The politics of recognition of others' identity includes an *emotional* element that *was not* present in the neutral, rational discourse of the traditional form of toleration. It can be a positive one: *sympathy* with other's cultural identity, and a negative one: *compassion* with others' *endangered* identity, in the form of their *offended pride*. In the end of my recent paper, I have mentioned the system of ideas of the contemporary *politics of recognition* as a possible solution of the emotional problem of the classical program of toleration (Mester 2016).

In the present writing of mine, I will analyse several aspects of the possibility of a new concept of toleration within the framework of *politics of recognition*, connected with the points of view of the values and elements of the cultural identity of people tolerated by us, focussed on the question of the connection of different *religious, cultural* and *political* identities, from the historical point of view, with several consequences for the present. In the following, *at first* I will outline the central idea of the relationship between the members of a religious community and the earthly power in the Jewish–Christian tradition, and its consequences for the European modernity. In the *second* chapter, I will offer an analysis of the religious toleration in its traditional form, concerning the structure of the states and religious communities, where the classical toleration is possible. In the *third* section, I will shortly show the roots of the concept of *recognition*, and a tension between the seemingly pre-modern features of forms of the collective identity emerged in several forms of *politics of recognition*, and modern requirements of the classical form of the religious toleration. In the *fourth* part of my writing I will outline the consequences of the *nostalgia* for an imagined pre-modern human condition in the nowadays popular vindication of the *rethinking* our own (European) *identity*. In the *fifth* and last part, I will formulate the demand of *rethinking* of the classical concept of toleration within the new circumstances of *politics of recognition*, making a distinction between the toleration concerning individuals and communities, saving the basic methodological individualism of the original theory of toleration connected with the classical social contract theories, and several anthropologies hidden behind them.

Believers and citizens in the Jewish–Christian tradition

However, there are numerous interpretations of the parallelism of the structure of the religious and political communities. Religious interpretations of the relationship between the believers and the earthly power are characterised by a clear distinction of the *civic* and *religious* aspect of the human nature, in the Jewish–Christian tradition. Both the *New Testament* and the *Babylonian Talmud* formulate the same civic obedience toward religiously alien earthly powers, the Babylonian and Roman Empires.[1] Experiences of the long *alien status* in states under pagan rulers have determined the political thought of the Jewish–Christian tradition, and have restricted the politically relevant part of the personality of the believers. In the beginning, there is no political community in this tradition;

1 For the most important Scriptural references see: Rom 13:1; 1 Pt 2:11–17. For the most significant Rabbinical locus see: Talmud: Gitin 10a. “dina d’malchuta dina”; (the law of the country [where you live] is a law [for you, as well]).

believers are the members of a religious community; and – as individuals – are *partly* subjected unto the earthly power, incarnated in a pagan person.

By the 16th-century Hungarian Protestant formulation of the same idea our *bodies* and *souls* are subjected unto the earthly power, not our *spirit*; and we have obligation for the estimation of the *office* of the ruler, not his *person*.[2] This restriction of the relationship between the person of the ruler and the persons of the subjected people conducts to the modern conceptions of the *institutionally mediated* political power and civic obedience known from the centuries of the early modernity in the European history of political ideas. Based on Augustinian ideas, the idea about the *distinction* between the *religious* and *political* communities, and the differences between the natures of our memberships in these communities has emerged. Difficult choices between the religious, national and local, civic identities, made under conditions of religious, civil wars and the fight against the Turkish Empire have trained the European mind to make clear distinction between the affairs of the political and religious entities. European citizens have learnt to recognise their fellow-citizen in the believer of an alien denomination, the political enemy of the nation in a believer of the same denomination, or the ally of the nation in a pagan, against Christian enemies.[3] This structured system of the functions of the political and religious communities, and the status of the individuals as citizens and as believers in the same time is the fundament of the European model of the political rule, and civic obedience. In this model, it is impossible to regard either the political or the religious community as a ruler of the *whole person* of their members. An intrinsic element of this system is the *institutional mediation* of the political power, and a neutral, rational analysis of the questions of the political and religious identity.

Prerequisites of the classical form of toleration

The classical form of toleration, based on the above discussed European system of the distinction between political and religious communities on the one hand, and between citizens and believers on the other, presupposes a special, limited

2 See Melius 1563. Despite its title, *Sermons in Hungarian*, it is a complete translation of the *Epistle to the Romans* with commentaries. Petrus Melius has established his abovementioned interpretation of the earthly power on the first words of Rom 13:1: "let *every soul* be subject unto the higher powers". See for the details my recent article (Mester 2015a).

3 For example, by the evidence of as early document of the Hungarian Protestantism, as the Confession approved in 1562.

structure and functioning both of the political and religious communities. A form of the early modern state, which did not want to rule over all the segments of the life of its citizens, could tolerate the religious practices of the members of a religious community which had gave up the total control over the everyday life of its citizens, at least, tacitly. The most influential theoretical formulation of this kind of toleration in the early modernity was *A Letter Concerning Toleration* by John Locke. (For an overview of its context, see Horton–Mendus 2004.) Locke's model presupposes that neither the earthly power, nor the church leaders want a religiously homogeneous country; and they do not touch a part of the identities of their subjects. The state is neutral, concerning the faith of their citizens; and the church is neutral, as well, concerning the civic identity of its believers, concerning different states. The possibility of the position of the theoretician as an *uninterested spectator* is based on the same structure; he (Locke) can see the believers from the point of view of the state, or the citizens from the point of view of the church (for my recent, detailed analysis of the question of early modern toleration, see Mester 2016).

The limits of this kind of the neutrality of the state have become clear when the requirement of the extension of the neutrality for the elements of the cultural, ethnical and linguistic elements of the collective identity has emerged in the multicultural societies, and the idea of the *ethnically neutral state* proved to be a utopia in the most cases. For the first glance, the distinction between the religious and ethnical neutrality of the state is an essential question. By a more detailed inquiry, we can learn to make distinction between different forms of both religious and ethnic entities, with different consequences for the structure of the state. For example, in the modern history of Switzerland we can observe a gradual, peaceful restructuration of the cantonal borders. In their initial form, cantons were *religiously* homogeneous, but in several cases *ethnically* heterogeneous political entities. Later, they have transformed to *ethnically* homogeneous, but *religiously* heterogeneous entities. Transformation of the internal structure of Switzerland mirrors two different historical statuses of the religious and ethnic identities in their relationship with the political community. In the initial form, a canton as a political entity cannot be neutral from a religious aspect, but it can be neutral from an ethnic aspect. Later, the situation is *vice versa*. The status of the religious and ethnic communities must be changed in the self-identification of the Swiss citizens on the one hand, and the daily tasks of the political community, on the other. When any church cannot regulate the daily life of the believers, and the management of the modern society requires a well-developed bureaucracy in native languages, political powers can be religiously neutral, but cannot be ethnically neutral.

Several problems of the *politics of recognition* and the concept of *recognition*

A widespread answer for the problems of the contemporary state concerning its required but hardly fulfilled cultural neutrality is the formulation of the political community as *community of communities*. In this framework there are new *moral* (actually: political) *subjects* between the individual citizens and the state (for a classic, theoretical proposal within this system of ideas, see Dyke 1977). They are mainly *ethnic minority groups*, but all communities, based on any *collective identity* are candidates for this political role. A common core of the arguments for the status of a moral subject is a self-evidence of the existence of these groups. The requirement of the recognition of these new-model moral subjects presupposes an imagined substantiality of these communities with the attribution of their *pre-existence* in comparison with the states.[4] This system of ideas clearly follows premodern patterns of the structure of the political power when an ancient empire had required the recognition of its supremacy, but the rule over the everyday life remained the territory of the *local tribal* or *religious* leaders.

Modern examples for the recognition of different collective identities often require the recognition of new, collective moral entities *within* a state. A possible political consequence in the *third world* is a conservation of the political power of a premodern, especially tribal native aristocracy with the protection of a modern state. A conservation of the power of the rulers is not the conservation of the premodern structure, and functions of their native communities. Accident elements of a premodern culture are used as the tools of the politics of recognition under conditions of the modernity. The requirement of the recognition of *whole* cultural communities as *moral entities*, and the new form of toleration derived from it is contrary to the European traditional model of toleration based on the separated spheres of identity. In this case, the elements of a cultural identity, which were non-political ones before, must be recognised politically. In this framework, it must be sacrificed the neutrality of the state, and toleration.

If we have a look at the roots of the possible frame-theory of the program of recognition of communities as moral subjects, namely, at the theory of recogni-

4 The present interpretation of the question of the ethnic groups as *moral subjects* is based on the conclusions of my contribution in a research project about the philosophy of *minority rights*. Fort he summarised conslusions of this project (in Hungarian) see Demeter 2007.

tion; we can realise a tension between the *theory of recognition*, and its several application in the *politics of recognition*.[5] However, the term of *recognition* has penetrated into the political philosophy as early as its Hegelian roots; it was originally a solution of an epistemological problem,[6] and concluded to the sphere of inter-subjectivity, and not to the inter-cultural relations. It seems that several modern applications of the *theory of recognition* in the *politics of recognition* have given up the feed-beck to the individuality. In the origins, the term of *recognition* was a tool for the individual self-understanding; in the end, the endeavour for the *recognition of communities* can be a tool for the annihilation of individuality.

Return to the (what kind of?) roots in Europe

In this situation has emerged the requirement of rethinking of the traditional model of toleration and the neutrality of state as twin ideas of the European modernity. The nowadays often repeated slogan of "return to the roots of the European identity" is based on this dilemma, as well. We can observe a special form of *nostalgia* for a kind of the values of an *imagined* premodern community. In this idea, we should *restructure* the European *identity* after the model of the values of the communities that demand the recognition as moral subjects within a political community. From the presupposed substantiality of these communities, their presupposed pre-existence in comparison with the state and their analogies with the premodern communities follows a model of a *closed society*, which offers a deterministic environment for the individuals who as the members of substantial, essential communities can play a strictly determined role in society. Under these conditions, a free self-identification of the individuals is impossible similarly to the restructuration of the collective identities, being substantial, natural ones. In this restructured European identity derived from the *nostalgia* of as "natural" form of identity of an imagined pre-modern community; in this *utopia*, values of a political community must be equal with the values of several religious or cultural communities. Rediscovering and recognition of several values as fundaments of the political community means that there is no difference between the cultural and political identities, memberships of *religious, cultural* and *political* communities must be equivalent. It is clear that both these structures of the in-

5 In the question of the roots of the modern theory of recognition, I have consulted Weiss 2004.

6 For a possible common Hegelian root of the *theory of recognition* and the *other minds problem* in the philosophy of mind see Zemach 1970, 369–370.

dividuals and the earthly power, and their relationships, as well, are *definitely contrary* to the Jewish–Christian tradition of the relationship of the believers and citizens described above, in the *first* section.

Instead of a conclusion: the demand to reformulate the concept of toleration and save the (methodologic) individualism

The initial problem of the present writing was an *emotional defect* of the classical concept of the European toleration, formulated as a lack of sympathy and compassion. We have outlined the roots of this concept and we have found it in the idea of the Jewish–Christian tradition about the relationship between the *political*, and *religious communities*, and between the *believer*, and *citizen* in the same person. Later, we have seen the endeavours for the rethinking of this formulation, with their consequences for the European identity, and the role of individuality in it. As a conclusion, we should declare the requirement of the return to the *contractual* basis of the political community balanced by a corrected form of the *politics of recognition*. A solution of the *emotional effect* of the classical concept of *toleration* cannot be linked with the cancellation of the *European* difference of the *cultural, religious*, and *political* identities. The priority between them must be based on an *individual* choice.[7]

References

Assmann, J. 2010. *Religio Duplex. Ägyptische Mysterien und europäische Aufklärung.* Berlin: Insel.

Demeter, M. A. 2007. *Egyén, állam, közösség [Individual, State, and Community].* Kolozsvár: Pro Philosophia. (*Műhely [Workshop]*; XV.)

Dyke, V. van 1977: The Individual, the State, and Ethnic Communities in Political Theory, *World Politics*, 29(3): 343–369.

Horton, J. & Mendus, S. (eds.) 2004: *John Locke: A Letter Concerning Toleration in Focus.* London – New York: Routledge.

Melius, P. 1563. *Magiar Praedikatioc, kit Postillanac neveznec [Hungarian Sermons, or Postilla].* Döbröcönbe: Töröc Mihál, RMK [Ancient Hungarian Library] I. 53, RMNy [Ancient Printings in Hungary] 194.

7 There is no place here to explain a detailed argumentation. Generally, I uphold my opinions formulated within the framework of the abovementioned Hungarian project (see Mester 2007).

Mester, B. 2007. *A kontraktualizmus védelmében. A kollektív jogok visszavezethetősége az egyéni jogokra [In Defence of Contractualism. A Derivation of the Collective Rights from the Individual Rights].* In Demeter 2007, pp. 70–81.

Mester, B. 2014. Th. Hobbes' visible rhetoric. A case study of history of political ideas. *Creativity Studies,* 7(2): 98–107.

Mester, B. 2015. The Concept of *Religio Duplex* within the Today Discourse of Globalisation. In: Dobrinescu, Anca (ed.) *The Dialogue of Cultures*, Ploieşti: Publishing House of Petroleum-Gas University of Ploieşti, pp. 155–165.

Mester, B. 2015a. The Scriptures in Hungarian in Early Modernity. *European Review: Interdisciplinary Journal of the Academia Europaea,* 23(3): 321–331.

Mester, B. 2016. From Erastianism to Irenism. Different Ways of Peace of the Religions in the Early Modern Europe. In: Juhant, J. & Žalec, B. (eds.), *Which Religion, What Ideology? The (religious) potentials for peace and violence,* Münster: Lit Verlag, pp. 87–95.

Weiss, J. 2004. *Az elismerés elmélete [A Theory of Recognition].* Budapest: Áron.

Zemach, E. M. 1970. Sensation, Raw Feels, and Other Minds. In: Buford, Th. O. (ed.), *Essays on Other Minds*, Urbana–Chicago–London, pp. 345–370.

"IT IS POSSIBLE TO ATTAIN TRUTH THROUGH A WAY PAVED BY LIES" – THE HISTORICAL TRAJECTORY OF COMMUNISM FROM COMPASSION AND TRUTH-SEEKING TO THE TOTALITARIAN TERROR

Gábor Kovács, Budapest

Introduction

1989, it is said to be a year of miracles; it is of course an allusion to the unexpected, really miracle-like collapse of the communism in Central-Eastern Europe. After more than a quarter of a century after this joyful event, it seems yet to be a relevant question: What was this cruel political system? There were certainly numerous interpretations at the time, when the inspected phenomenon was an alive and robust reality. These explanative schemes can be divided into different types. First, concentrating on the structure of that political arrangement, it can be said that it was an extremely cruel tyranny, based upon, at least in the first phase of its existence, systematic and conscious exertion of terror (Arendt 1967). Additionally, the functionalist explanation is a popular approach among historians in the present time; from the dominant economic perspective it lends itself so to say naturally: communism was an unsuccessful ideology of modernization promising a quick catching up for backward regions in Central-Eastern Europe and in Asia.

Ernest Gellner gave a sociological explanation focusing on the special historical-social and political situation of Central and Eastern Europe. Hannah Arendt produced a philosophical explication, raising the question: how was it possible that Marxian emancipatory philosophy, the heir of the Enlightenment, begot a terroristic totalitarian political system as the Stalinist socialism? According to her explanation, impersonal pity, which was one of the main motives of Jacobin revolutionaries, the predecessors of Bolsheviks, involved a contempt of real, concrete individual human life, and led to the sacrifice of it for the sake of abstract, inhuman ideals (Arendt 1990).

Communism as a pseudo-religion

To interpret communism as a pseudo-religion promising this-worldly salvation was a widely applied scheme of explanation from the beginning. Nikolai Berdyaev, in his book on the origin and essence of communism, traced back this phenomenon to the peculiarities of Russian history and culture: he emphasized the importance of Russian Messianism deeply rooted in the collective psyche:

"The religious formation of the Russian spirit developed several stable attributes: dogmatism, asceticism, the ability to endure suffering and to make sacrifices for the sake of its faith whatever that may be, a reaching out to the transcendental, in relation now to eternity, to the other world, now to the future, to this world. The religious energy of the Russian spirit possesses the faculty of switching over and directing itself to purposes that are not merely religious, for example, to social objects. In virtue of their religious-dogmatic quality of spirit, Russians – whether orthodox, heretics or schismatics – are always apocalyptic or nihilist" (Berdyaev, *The Origin of Russian Communism*, 3-4).

What is of importance for us from the perspective of this paper is the conclusion from the last chapter from his book concerning the deeply hostile attitude of communism to religion in general and Christianity in particular case:

"Communism in actual fact is the foe of every form of religion and especially of Christianity, not as a social system, but as itself a religion. It wants to be a religion itself, to take the place of Christianity. It professes to answer the religious questions of the human soul and to give a meaning to life. Communism is integrated; it embraces the whole of life; its relations are with no special section of it. On this account, its conflict with other religious faiths is inevitable. Intolerance and fanaticism always have a religious origin. No scientific, purely intellectual theory can be so intolerant and fanatical, and communism is exclusive as a religious faith is" (Berdyaev, *The Origin of Russian Communism*, 106-107).

It can be rightly said that communism was not only a Russian phenomenon; there was a strong affinity to it in other parts of the world, and this is undeniably a relevant objection. In the interpretation of Mircea Eliade, neither the Russian history and collective psyche nor the special Russian messianistic attitude attributing to Russia the role of the redemptor of the whole world are the main cause of the quasi-religious character of the communist doctrine. It was Marx himself, whose thinking was tinted by religious prophetic overtones. Marxism, according to Eliade, is a secularized version of the ancient eschatological doctrines:

"Marx takes over and continues one of the great eschatological myths of the Asiatico-Mediterranean world-the redeeming role of the Just (the "chosen," the "anointed," the "innocent," the "messenger"; in our day, the proletariat), whose sufferings are destined to change the ontological status of the world. (…) It is even significant that Marx takes over for his own purposes the Judaeo-Christian eschatological hope of *an absolute end to history* (…)" (Eliade, *The Sacred and the Profane*, 101).

In the interpretation of Ernest Gellner, communism appears as a quasi-religious phenomenon, too, as a failed secularized *Ersatz-religion* promising salvation not to the individual, but to the whole mankind. It was, as the consequence of its collectivist perspective, unable, Gellner argues, to supply comfort and relief to an individual being in existential crisis (Gellner 1996, 39). Moreover, it did not separate the spheres of the sacred and profane; it sacralized everyday life, especially economic activity, not letting a neutral zone into which the individual could have receded after the diminution of the quasi-religious fervor of the communist doctrine, promising this-worldly salvation. However, the final cause of the collapse was its corruption, Gellner concludes, in a sarcastic manner:

"When the *nomenklatura* killed each other and accompanied the murderous rampage with blatantly mendacious political theatre, belief survived; but when the *nomenklatura* switched from shooting each other to bribing each other, faith evaporated. The squalor of the work relationship was the equivalent of corrupt priesthood in other faiths" (Gellner 1996, 41).

At the focal point of communism is power, more precisely the question concerning the seizing of political power. This approach inevitably leads to the problem of force and violence applied in political deed, and involves ethical dimension. Communist ethics gave answer to the ethical dilemmas of a communist believer committed to this this-worldly doctrine of a salvation within the framework of a historical philosophy in which evil goes through a miraculous transformation: it appears as good and desirable from the perspective of world history. However, this is a laicized version of the well-known dilemma of Christian theology: How can we accommodate the idea of an absolutely good God with the conspicuous fact of the existence of wickedness in human history? There is no room here to reconstruct the secularization of this excruciating religious dilemma, but it is worth dwelling for a moment at the famous scene of Goethe's Faust in which Faust requests Mephistopheles appearing in the shape of a dog to reveal his name:

"FAUST
What is thy name?
MEPHISTOPHELES
A question small, it seems,
For one whose mind the Word so much despises;
Who, scorning all external gleams,
The depths of being only prizes.
FAUST
With all you gentlemen, the name's a test,
Whereby the nature usually is expressed.
Clearly the latter it implies

In names like Beelzebub, Destroyer, Father of Lies.
Who art thou, then?
MEPHISTOPHELES
Part of that Power, not understood,
Which always wills the Bad, and always works the Good." (Goethe, *Faust*)
/translated by Bayard Taylor/

Arthur Koestler, a Hungarian origin writer, knew bolshevism from within. In his adventurous youth, he was one of the members of his generation who was not able to resist the temptation of the communism promising this worldly salvation and joined the communist party. Later he lost his faith and became a fervent anti-communist. His famous book, entitled *Darkness at noon* (1940) was the evidence of his disillusionment. The book had been inspired by the bloody puppet show of show trials of Moscow against the former party leaders, Kamenev and Zinoviev in 1936. In the conversation between the arrested Rubashov, a former high ranked Bolshevik leader, and his interrogator, Ivanov Koestler, he gave a brilliant description of an inhuman ideological attitude that considers concrete human beings as mere means in the service of a cruel utopian aim, and finds the moral justification of force and violence in their alleged good end-consequences. Ivanov, the interrogator, gives - in a cynical-derisive manner - his arrested comrade a short lecture on the relation of ethics and the communist historical philosophy based on the idea of historical necessity:

"I would like to write a Passion in which God and the Devil dispute for the soul of Saint Rubashov. After a life of sin he has turned to God – to a God with the double chin of industrial liberalism and the charity of the Salvation Army soups. Satan, on the contrary, is thin, ascetic, and a fanatical devotee of logic. He reads Machiavelli, Ignatius of Loyola, Marx, and Hegel; he is cold and unmerciful to mankind, out of a kind of mathematical mercifulness. He is damned always to do that which is most repugnant to him: to become a slaughterer in order to abolish slaughtering; to sacrifice lambs so that no more lambs may be slaughtered; to whip people with knouts so that may learn not to let themselves be whipped; to strip himself of every scruple in the name of a higher scrupulousness; and to challenge the hatred of mankind because of his love for it – an abstract and geometric love" (Koestler 1994, 122).

Koestler's reconstruction of the communist conceptualization of the problems of ethics is not only a fiction, a product of literary fantasy; the case of Georg Lukács expressly proves it. Lukács was, in the years preceding the WWI, a promising young philosopher and aesthetician, feeling himself home both in Hungarian and German culture. He was a member of the Weber-circle in Heidelberg with such prominent intellectuals as Karl Jaspers and Ernst Bloch. The breaking out of the war had upset his world-view; his old discontent with the banality of the "bourgeois world culminated in a deep personal crisis: he felt life unbearable, using the famous term of Fichte, in the world of absolute sinfulness. Joining the Hungarian Communist Party and taking a political role in the short-lived Hungarian Soviet Republic in the end of 1918 and in the first months of 1919 seemed to him as an escape from this crisis; as a solution to his exacerbating dilemmas, as a possible anchor in a disintegrating world. His intellectual background varied: German idealism, existence-philosophies, Jewish messianism, Dostoevsky, Marx, Russian anarchism – these were its main components. His religious-like conversion to communism was a surprise for his close friends. In December 1918, soon before his joining the communist party, he wrote an essay entitled *Bolshevism as a moral problem*. The starting point of his thought-train is symptomatic, reflecting a deep ethical sensitivity: "[t]he decision for or against Bolshevism (…) has to be an ethical one" (Lukács 1977, 418). The essence of this ethical decision stands very clearly before him: "(…) we are faced with the following moral dilemma: If we take advantage of the given possibility for the realization of our goal, we have to accept dictatorship, terror and the class oppression that goes with it. The existing class oppression will then have to be replaced by that of proletariat – to drive out Satan – with the help of Beelzebub, so to speak (…)" (Lukács 1977: 422) The text is abundant in religious allusions and terms: "credo quia absurdum" "redemptive role" etc. There is an insoluble opposition, Lukács argues, between individual moral consciousness and responsibility and the ultimate goal, this-worldly salvation of mankind by the collective Messiah, the proletariat. There is an inherent paradox of this situation: whatever you choose, you have to commit sin. In this point of his argumentation, Lukács lifts into his train of thought the notion of self-sacrifice: it means to sacrifice the personal moral clearness in the altar of the ultimate goal. It is seems to him unacceptable: in the end of his essay, he declares that he is unable to do this last step and consequently refuses Bolshevism:

"(…) Bolshevism rests on the metaphysical assumption that the bad can endanger the good, or as Razumikhin says in Dostoevsky's Crime and Punishment, that it is possible to lie our way through to the truth.

This author is unable to share this belief. Accordingly, he perceives an insoluble moral problem at the root of the Bolshevik standpoint" (Lukács 1977, 424).

After some month of this conclusion, Lukács wrote another essay entitled *Tactics and ethics*. At that moment, he had been after an existential decision: he became a member of Hungarian Communist Party. We do not have direct evidence for the reconstruction of psychological transformation of Lukács: he did not write diary in which he would have illuminated the moving springs of this metamorphosis. There are debates about the nature of this event. Some interpreters emphasize the quasi-religious nature of this change; they point out to the unexplainable discontinuity in his thought and write about conversion. Other interpreters, to the contrary see continuity in his thought in this respect; the joining the communist party, according to them, can be described as an intellectual evolution, as the consequence of long deliberative thinking process.

However, when Lukács wrote *Tactics and ethics* he was already on the other shore of Rubicon: he had become a communist being already able to sacrifice personal ethics in the altar of the ultimate objective defined by the communist party. He was conscious of the consequences of his decision, but he was already able to accept the "logic of history" deduced from the Marxian historical philosophy. Ethics must be subordinated to the tactics determined by the actual situation of a class struggle. The ultimate objective, a communist society, had been invested with the quality of an immanent, this-worldly soteriological endpoint by him. This, according to Lukács, is not merely a utopia; the prerequisites of it could be deduced from world history. The requirements of the communist party tactics overwrite the personal moral conviction of the party member. At the same time, in a deeply paradox manner, Lukács in this point of his train thought does not give up his moral point of view, the agent can't be relieved from the burden of individual moral decision. He does not eliminate ethical responsibility; quite the contrary, he extends its terrain to an extreme manner:

"Everyone who at the present time opts for communism is therefore obliged to bear the same *individual* responsibility for each and every human being who dies for him in the struggle, as if he himself had killed them all. But all those who ally themselves to the other side, the defence of capitalism, must bear the same individual responsibility for the destruction entailed in the new imperialist revanchist wars which are surely imminent, and for the future oppression of the nationalities and classes." (Lukács 1975:10)

There is no other escape, according to Lukács, than the last self-sacrifice of the moral agent as a moral agent, which had been rejected by him some months earlier. There is a tragic situation in which decision inevitably involves guilty: if you follow the inviolable prescription of individual moral action concerning the prohibition of killing you'll become an accomplice because of the later consequences of your decision resulting in innocent victims killed by one(s) whom you failed to kill. What to do? There is no solution, there is no absolution: you are not able to avoid the state of sinfulness. But, Lukács writes, rather surprisingly, there is a standard of correct action in this tragic and unhopeful situation:

"This standard we call sacrifice. And just as the individual who chooses between two forms of guilt finally makes the correct choice when he sacrifices his inferior self on the altar of the higher idea (…)" (Lukács 1975, 10).

Conclusion

So, you do not have choice, except to accept the inevitable guilty inherent in the act of choice and to take the responsibility of becoming a murderer if the requirements of the party tactics dictate it to you. Lukács formulates this gruesome conclusion by referring to the book of Boris Savinkov, a Russian terrorist who was the leader of a terrorist group in the Russian revolution of 1904–1906. It is a biblical allusion to the words of Judith killing Holofernes from the drama of the German writer Friedrich Hebbel:

"(…) murder is not allowed, it is an absolute and unpardonable sin; it 'may' not, but yet it 'must' be committed. Elsewhere in the same book he sees, not the justification (that is impossible) but the ultimate moral basis of the terrorist's act as the sacrifice for his brethren, not only of his life, but also of his purity, his morals, his very soul. In other words, only he who acknowledges unflinchingly and without any reservations that murder is under no circumstances to be sanctioned can commit the murderous deed that is truly — and tragically — moral. To express this sense of the most profound human tragedy in the incomparably beautiful words of Hebbel's Judith: 'Even if God had placed sin between me and the deed enjoined upon me — who am I to be able to escape it?'" (Lukács 1975, 11).

This paper was supported by the Hungarian Scientific Research Fund (OTKA K104643).

References

Arendt, H. 1967. *The Origins of Totalitarianism*. Cleveland and New York: The World Publishing Company.

Arendt, H. 1990. *On Revolution*: London: Penguin Books.

Berdyaev, N. *The Origin of Russian Communism*. Translated from Russian by R. M. French. London: The University Press 1948 (1937); http://www.jesus-for-all.com/fikr/pdf_3189.pdf (accesed January 1, 2015).

Eliade, M. *The Sacred and the Profane*. Translated from the French by Willard R. Trask A Harvest Book Harcourt, Brace & World, Inc. New York; https://www.dmt-nexus.me/doc/the%20sacred%20and%20the%20profane.pdf (accessed September 10, 2015).

Gellner, E. 1996. *The Conditions of Liberty*. London: Penguin Books, 1996.

Goethe, J. W. *Faust*. http://www.gutenberg.org/files/14591/14591-h/14591-h.htm#I (accessed September 10, 2015).

Koestler, A. 1994. *Darkness at Noon*. Translated by Daphne Hardy. London: Vintage.

Lukács, G. 1975. *Tactics and Ethics*: political essays, 1919-1929. Translated from the German by Michael McColgan ; edited, with an introd., by Rodney Livingstone, New York : Harper & Row.

Lukács, G. 1977. Bolshevism as a Moral Problem. *Social Research* 44(3): 416–424.

GEORGES FLOROVSKY AND RUSSIAN INTELLECTUAL HISTORY: REJECTION OF ORTHODOXY AS A WAY TOWARDS THE BOLSHEVIK REVOLUTION?

Simon Malmenvall, Ljubljana

Introduction

The author of this article aims at presenting the historiographical-philosophical views of Georges Florovsky (1893–1979), Russian Orthodox emigrant theologian, philosopher and historian. Florovsky's views originate in the normativity of patristic theology and argue that from the 16th century onwards the Russian thought (both Orthodox and secular) was "in captivity" imposed by the Western influences. As a consequence, several obscure intellectual movements or "dead ends" emerged, including the Bolshevik revolution in 1917. The author of this article, focusing primarily on the narrative of the *Ways of Russian Theology* (one of Florovsky's main works), accepts the views of Florovsky as reasonable, yet at the same time partial. Firstly, these views are concerned with the long-term intellectual reasons for the rise of Bolshevism, without taking into consideration the complexity of both political and economic situation at the turn of 19–20th century. Secondly, they do not only form the basic notions for the understanding of the Russian intellectual and ecclesiastical history, but also represent a treatise on how to built the desired future of universal Orthodoxy in general.

Life of Georges Florovsky

A theologian, philosopher and historian Georges Vasilievich Florovsky (1893–1979) belongs to the group of the greatest Russian thinkers. Together with Vladimir Lossky, Sergey Bulgakov and Justin Popović, Florovsky is regarded as the leading Orthodox theologian of the 20th century. In the initial period of his exile following the civil war in the former Russian Empire, he became a professor at the Paris Orthodox Theological Institute of St. Serge, where he dedicated himself to the study of the Eastern Church fathers and Russian intellectual and ecclesiastical history. After the Second World War, he moved to the United States. As a professor, he worked in the Orthodox Theological Seminary of Saint Vladimir, at the Harvard University and at the end of his career at the Princeton University. He was one of the founders of the ecumenical World Council of Churches and a member of the American Academy of Sciences. His leading works *Eastern Fathers of the 4th century* (1931) and *Ways of Russian theology* (1937) have become a must-have reference point for anyone embarking on a journey of acquainting oneself with Orthodox spirituality and culture.[1]

Context of Florovsky's thought

The context of the later, mature Florovsky's works is formed by relativization of importance of the Russian religious "renaissance" at the end of the 19th and beginning of the 20th century, which is especially evident in the implicit criticism of its founder, philosopher Vladimir Solovyov (1853–1900). According to Florovsky, the religious "renaissance" was the cause for weakening of the loyalty to the official Orthodox doctrine and increased dependence of modern Russian philosophy on the Western influences, mainly on German idealist philosophy. (Florovskij 1983, 250–253; 308; 310–318; 320–321; 463–464; 466; 492–493; Gavrilyuk 2014, 98–99; 106–112; 143; 182; 229; 263; Raeff 1993, 255–257; 272–274)

Essential elements of Florovsky's thought are best summarized in the concept of neopatristic synthesis or Christian Hellenism, which can be understood as a kind of Orthodox "philosophia perennis" – the Christian view, surpassing individual cultures, originating in the reflections of the Church fathers of the 1st millennium. In Christian Hellenism the Church doctrine and historical experience of God are closely intertwined – God, according to the Biblical pattern, speaks to each individual in person, that is via integration of an individual in the Church and also his ethical decision-making in relation to the world. According to Florovsky, the Christian faith as a whole, owing to the Sacred Scripture, is an heir to the Jewish way of thinking, while at the same time – due to the late-antiquity definitions of the Church fathers – being indelibly marked by the Hellenic conceptualisations. It is precisely the historicity of Divine revelation that gives sense to the tradition as an essential ontological component forming the Church. This is due to the fact that through variability of historical circumstances the tradition is supposed to holistically explain the "eternal truths" again and again. These truths, resting in the inseparable relationship between the Bible and the Church fathers, the apostolic period and the subsequent history of the Church, always reflect the continuity of acting of the Holy Spirit in the Church. Thus, the patristic theology in Florovsky's view always represents a norm, according to which any subsequent philosophical or theological movement should be judged.

1 The present biographical account is summarized from a detailed study on Florovsky's professional and private life by Andrew Blane (Blane 1993).

(Florovskij 1983, 506–507; 509; 511–513; Gavrilyuk 2014, 5; 96–97; 112; 125; 150–151; 201–202; 204; 206–207; 211–215; 222–224; Williams 1993, 289–291; 322–324)

Neopatristic synthesis, according to Florovsky's understanding, should not take a form of a restoration of the past – he wanted the patristic theology to become actual and credible in any circumstances. Believing in non-withered freshness of the Orthodox tradition, Florovsky saw Protestant and modern thought, originating in the Enlightenment, as narrow-minded and somewhat qucikly passing. With this in mind, Florovsky can be characterized as an "innovative traditionalist", as someone who creatively linked the tradition of the Church to the dilemmas of his time without exposing the tradition to the historical relativization (Florovskij 1983, 506–507; 513; Gavrilyuk 2014, 1; 10–11; 69–70; 96–97; 125; 214–216; 219).

Ways of Russian Theology and a long way towards Bolshevism

Florovsky's call to the neopatristic synthesis or Christian Hellenism in his *Ways of Russian Theology* (*Puti russkogo bogosloviya*) is based on the synthetical review and evaluation of the Russian intellectual history. The examples from the Russian environment – that is, something "partial" – served as means to implement something "universally" ecclesiastical. (Florovskij 1983, 506–507; 509; 511–513; Raeff 1993, 261) The core of Florovsky's *Ways of Russian Theology* is represented by the position that from the 16th century onwards the Russian Orthodox theology – and also secular thought – became "imprisoned" by the Western influences: initially the Catholic ones via the intervention of Orthodox as well as Unionist intellectuals hailing from the territory of present-day Ukraine and Belarus, later by the Protestant and those of the Enlightenment, and lastly by the idealistic ones. According to Florovsky, this caused the Russian thought as a whole not only to lose its identity, but above all to produce a series of "pseudomorphoses" affecting Russian Orthodoxy, wasting its loyalty to the patristic and Byzantine theology in effect. The rejection of the tradition of the Church fathers, encouraged by the religious nationalism of the Muscovite State rising from the effort to refrain from the Greek "treacherousness" after their temporary acceptance of the Florentine ecclesiastical union with Rome (1439) and fall of Constantinople (1453), occurred no later than at the beginning of the 16th century, only to deepen afterwards. (Florovskij 1983, 24–28; 49; 56; 77; 81–84; 97–98; 104–105; 107; 117–119; 149–150; 200–201; 252–253; 285–288; 294; 330; 404–409; 412–413; 432–433; 450–451; 454–456; 492–500; 502–505) According to Florovsky, the rise of the mentioned religious nationalism was made possible by the final defeat of the "Volga elders" monastic movement ("zavolzhskyie startsy") during the rule of Ivan the Terrible (1547–1584). In this regard, the vision of the socially active Christianity, supported by the secular power of the Muscovite state, prevailed over its contemplative vision, which was rooted in the patristic-Byzantine tradition (Florovskij 1983, 9–12; 17–28).

The interpretation of the Russian intellectual and ecclesiastical history as observed in Florovsky's work originates in the principles of traditional Orthodox ecclesiology, according to which the credibility of individual theologians and thinkers depends also on their involvement in the liturgical-sacramental and ascetic life of the Church – in other words, on a quality of their "Christian way of life". The entire interpretation made by Florovsky rests on a commitment to the experience and tradition of the Church, which – thanks to the ever-present intervention of the Holy Spirit – should be seen as the final measure of the truth. (Florovsky 1972, 58–59; 60–61; Raeff 1993, 253–254; 257–258; 268–269; Williams 1993, 294; 308–309) This explains why Florovsky in his *Ways of Russian Theology* so often stops at the "tragedy" of the Russian Orthodox Church and "dead ends" of the Russian culture. The gradual transition from the Muscovite religious nationalism to the idealist philosophy, and finally to the Bolshevik revolution was, according to Florovsky, made possible by disregard for the liturgical life of the Church by the Orthodox thinkers. This in turn led to the rise of the opposition between liturgy and theology, between religious practice and education causing the Church in the Russian society to gradually transform into an obsolete and reactionary institution. Being severed from the Church, theology and related philosophy became a reflection of arbitrarily understood "progress" with its utilitarian atheistic (eg. Herzen, Lenin) or theistic idealistic (eg. Khomyakov, Solovyov) "dead ends". (Florovskij 1983, 84; 92; 101; 201; 252–253; 311; 314; 316–318; 492–499; 502–505; Gavrilyuk 2014, 178–184; 220–222; 228-229; Raeff 1993, 267–269; 271)

As the only positive phenomenon in the Russian intellectual history after the 16th century, Florovsky acknowledges the "historical school" from the middle and second half of the 19th century. Florovsky regards this ideational current – despite being mainly secular and limited to a group of university scholars – with its publishing of the patristic works in Russian translation and thorough study of (Russian) history as the only one that could have hampered the strenghtening of the various "dead ends". Namely, it could have pointed at the senselessness of the utopistic social projects, enhanced the historical consciousness and affirmed the role of the ecclesiastical tradition. Regardless of its alleged potential, at the end of the 19th century this current was forced to give way to the popularity of the "religious renaissance" on one hand and the socialist ideas on the other. (Florovskij 1983, 335–339; 350–352; 364–367; 369–373; 382–386; 390–393; 400–413; 427–428; 450–451)

In this regard, the success of the Bolshevik revolution as the culmination of all the "dead ends" was decisively influenced by the inability of the Russian Orthodox Church to provide its own response to the complex societal challenges at hand and, consequently, strengthen complementarity between intellect and ecclesiastical life. The lack of responsiveness and creativity of the Russian Church is explained by Florovsky as the result of two main factors. On the one hand, the Russian Church was fatally undermined by the submission to the absolutist state at the time of Peter the Great (1689–1721), most notably by the abolition of the Moscow patriarchate and the establishment of the Holy Synod. On the other hand, the Russian Church was greatly affected by the actions of its intellectuals, who from the beginning of the 19th century often accepted principles of German idealist philosophy. By doing that – in the name of moral accountability to the society – they abused Christianity in search for a timeless utopia without taking into account the reality of the time, historical consciousness, Orthodox dogmas and canons, liturgical and ascetic traditions and, above all, without a firm faith in Christ as the sole saviour of the world (Florovskij 1983, 199–201; 235–236; 240–242; 250–253; 285–288; 291–292; 313–321; 331; 401; 408–413; 433; 450–451; 454–456; 483; 492–499; 502–514; Gavrilyuk 2014, 9; 57–59; 106–112; 150–151; 179–184; Raeff 1993, 250–251; 258; 263–264; 266–267; 271–274; 276).

Critical evaluation

Amnogst Florovsky's thesis the one about the fatal consequences of the separation between liturgical-sacramental life and intellectual activity is particularly insightful. The majority of the Russian Orthodox clergy, throughout centuries formed in a distinct pietistic and everyday-practical spirit, did not succeed in the attempt to make the dangers of the social problems and, above all, the utopistic projects as an inadequate answer to them evident to the wider portions of the population. It is the neglect of the theological aspects of the Christian faith, closely tied to the understanding of history and society, that seems to best explain the weakness of the Russian Orthodox Church in relation towards Bolshevism.

Despite his consistent line of argument, supported by a rich set of primary historical sources, Florovsky's thought calls for some additional explanations and partly also criticism in at least two major points. Firstly, the understanding of long-term reasons for the outbreak of the Bolshevik revolution by Florovsky is perfectly acceptable only at the level of intellectual history, while the other reasons (such as economic and political) contributing to a holistic historical account, remain completely neglected. In this regard, it is particularly important not to omit the devastating consequences of World War I, the striking inequality of the population, failed agrarian reform, public debt, weakening of the central government due to the unsuccessful gradual democratization (Annanich 2006, 410–411; 417–418; 422–423; Shakibi 2006, 434; 446–448; Lohr 2006, 655–656; 659–669; Steinberg 2006, 68–69; 72; 82–85, 87–89).

Secondly, contrary to the Florovsky's view, the Russian Church throughout its history did not neglect intellectual activity as such, but rather its predominant orientation was different from the patristic-Byzantine, ideas of which were close to that of Florovsky. Therefore, by recalling the past "tragedy" Florovsky offers his own perspective (Christian Hellenism) on the development of the modern Orthodox philosophy and theology of the time. *Ways of Russian theology* – apart from being a work on the Russian intellectual and ecclesiastical history – represent, without a doubt, also a treatise on how to built the desired future of universal Orthodoxy in general (Gavrilyuk 2014, 11; 96–97; 166–167; 176–177; 190; Raeff 1993, 261; Florovskij 1983, 506–507; 509; 511–513).

Conclusion

The complementarity of historical review and treatise on the future of Orthodoxy forms the essence of Florovsky's approach regarding the Russian intellectual and ecclesiastical history (with its many "dead ends") in general and the reasons for the success of the Bolshevik revolution (as the culmination of all "dead ends") in particular. This approach is best reflected in the preface to the *Ways of Russian Theology*: "Studying the Russian past led me to the conviction and strengthened me in it that in our day the Orthodox theologian can only find for himself the true measure and living source of creative inspiration in patristic tradition. I am convinced the intellectual break from patristics and Byzantinism was the chief cause for all the interruptions and failures in Russia's development. […] That this narrow path of patristic theology is the sole true way is revealed with particular clarity in historical perspective. Yet the return to the fathers must not be solely intellectual or historical, it must be a return in spirit and prayer, a living and creative self-restoration to the fullness of the Church in the entirety of sacred tradition" (Florovsky 1979, VII).

References

Ananich, B. 2006. The Russian Economy and Banking System. In: *The Cambridge History of Russia. Volume II: Imperial Russia, 1689–1719*. Dominic Lieven, red. Cambridge: Cambridge University Press, pp. 394–425.

Blane, A. 1993. A Sketch of the Life of Georges Florovsky. In: *George Florovsky: Russian Intellectual and Orthodox Churchman*. Andrew Blane, red. Crestwood: St. Vladimir's Seminary Press, pp. 11–217.

Florovskij, G. V. 1983. *Puti russkogo bogosloviya*, 3rd edition. Paris: YM-CA-Press.

Florovsky, G. 1972. The Church: Her Nature and Task. In: *Collected Works of Georges Florovsky. Volume 1: Bible, Church, Tradition: An Eastern Orthodox View*, Belmont: Norland Publishing Company, pp. 57–72.

Florovsky, Georges. 1979. *Ways of Russian Theology, Part One (Collected Works of Georges Florovsky, Volume V).* Robert L. Nichols, trans. Belmont: Norland Publishing Company.

Gavrliyuk, P. L. 2014. *Georges Florovsky and the Russian Religious Renaissance.* Oxford: Oxford University Press.

Lohr, E. 2006. War and Revolution, 1914–1917. In: *The Cambridge History of Russia. Volume II: Imperial Russia, 1689–1719.* Dominic Lieven, red. Cambridge: Cambridge University Press, pp. 655–669.

Raeff, M. 1993. Enticements and Rifts: Georges Florovsky as Russian Intellectual Historian. In: *George Florovsky: Russian Intellectual and Orthodox Churchman.* Andrew Blane, red. Crestwood: St. Vladimir's Seminary Press, pp. 219–286.

Shakibi, Z. P. 2006. Central Government. In: *The Cambridge History of Russia. Volume II: Imperial Russia, 1689–1719.* Dominic Lieven, red. Cambridge: Cambridge University Press, pp. 429–448.

Steinberg, M. D. 2006. Russia's *fin de siècle*, 1900–1914. In: *The Cambridge History of Russia. Volume III: The Twentieth Century.* Ronald Grigor Suny, red. Cambridge: Cambridge University Press, pp. 67–93.

Williams, G. H. 1993. The Neo-Patristic Synthesis of Georges Florovsky. In: *George Florovsky: Russian Intellectual and Orthodox Churchman.* Andrew Blane, red. Crestwood: St. Vladimir's Seminary Press, pp. 287–340.

TRUTH AND COMPASSION ON THE HORIZON OF INTERPERSONAL RELATIONSHIPS AND PERSONAL RESPONSIBILITY

Mateja Pevec Rozman, Ljubljana

The notion of truth through postmodern perspective

There are numerous and often conflicting attempts to define truth in postmodernity. This paper does not attempt to examine and analyze all those approaches, since such a task is beyond the scope of this analysis.

Postmodernity describes a new approach in the social sciences that opposes systematical thinking that tries to unify everything – an approach that started with Descartes. Postmodernity does not think that such a systematic discourse is possible. It proposes radical plurality that turns all possible perspectives into relative perspectives and denounces an all-working center. Because of the influence of the advancement of informational technology, that accelerates the fragmentation of a unified discourse, this pluralism is more visible in modern industrial societies (Lyotard calls it metadiscourse).

An important characteristic of postmodern culture is the absence of any universal criterion of critical judgement. There is no clear distinction between right and wrong, or good and bad. The only criterion is the individual. The individual defines his or her criteria. He or she does so by relying on his or her personal feelings and intuitions that, combined with the individual's (personal) experiences, are then applied to individual phenomena. The current postmodern atmosphere is defined by a sense of relativism – a general lack of interest for the challenges of our time or lack of interest for the truth (Senegačnik 1998, 10–13). There is also a sense that the postmodern society has not yet established a strategy to define a common ground for all the differences (Juhant 1993, 126). Relativism denies the existence of a universal system of values that gives the individual a sense of certainty and gives "aid" in making decisions. We talk about moral relativism, when we discuss morality. Moral relativism refutes universal moral principles. Its proponents argue that the plurality of cultures, customs and moral priorities deny all attempts to define any universal moral principles.

The fact that values, chosen by each and every individual, cannot be examined, set an epistemological and moral tone. It limits the possibility of knowledge and makes it impossible to question or criticize one`s values. Everyone has the right to choose what is right and wrong, act accordingly, and except the consequences of his or her decisions. This is the foundation of the individual`s moral autonomy, that has to be respected. (MacNiven 2005, 2)

These characteristics, as well as indefiniteness and unintelligibility – postmodernity in its essence refuses any attempt to give a universal understanding, to find a common denominator, to find absolute truth, and leans toward plurality, choice and subjectivity – draw the picture of postmodernity. Postmodernity often advocates mutually exclusive concepts in a vast array of fields, like art, media, history, sociology, economy, politics, ethics, cosmology, theology, literature, education etc. (Jamnik 1998, 259).

The postmodern notion of reality

In the time of the crises of reason that began with the fall of the great ideologies (grand narratives), postmodernity finds itself in a position where we could renounce ourselves from the truth. Yet it seems as if postmodern literature pictures truth in the shape of a unified system, a network of connected concepts and an organic form for every phenomenon. "This notion of truth comes to life, because postmodernist derive it from the historical works of art, philosophy and science, which they then restore or repeat."(Kos 1995, 111). We might be witnessing the creation of a mosaic of truths that are not compatible and that compete with each other. All truths are possible. Even all truths at once are possible, and if they exist, they could all be truthful or they could all be mere appearances.

Postmodernity replaces the notion of a unified reality - a view that was the basis for an empirical conscience in modernity – with the plurality of differences. This "differences" can be real or artificial, they could be incompatible, and that is why meaning remains open, uncertain and ambiguous. If truths do not construct reality as a whole, but replace it, they render reality inaccessible. But, the abolishment of truth as a system is not the only difference between modernity and postmodernity. Modernity did not understand truth as a system either. In literature, for example, postmodernity does not only abolish truth, but denies that works of literature are capable of showing truth as a presence of the world that is accessible to our consciousness (Kos 1995, 116). Pluralities of truths emerge and they cannot be sorted in a hierarchical order. This leads to a coexistence of truths that make it possible for everyone to be "right", thus giving the impression of tolerance. This so called tolerance does not lead to a more harmonious interpersonal relationships. If there is no absolute truth that can be used to measure other attempts at the truth, truth becomes something one merely has. But there is no ultimate truth. If we were to discuss the question of the ultimate truth, we would be forced to ask the question of origin. But postmodernity defies all attempts of rediscovering the origin and opposes attempts to represent the origin or any origin of being or the underlying reality of the phenomena. Instead of that, postmodernity promotes doubt and denies the existence of the origin. (Jamnik 1998, 270) When there is no truth or there are several truths and everybody has "his or her own truth", can we talk about compassion? What is the object of compassion if compassion relies on the acceptance of truth? Which truth?

How can we find an answer in this chaos – the consequence of the plurality of truths or rather the abolishment of truth? The answer might be a constant effort to find the truth. But truth is not something that we could possess or own. Rather truth is something or someone that we belong to. The task of thinking, which is free and surpasses itself, is to serve the truth (Sorč 1999, 16-19).

Questioning reality (and the validity of truths) is not a concept that is foreign to postmodernity. It represents the crisis of postmodernity. And even that is not truly new. To demonstrate this, let us look at the modern philosopher René Descartes, who is regarded as the father of rationalism. In his book *Meditations on First Philosophy,* he writes:

"I will suppose then, that everything I see is spurious. I will believe that my memory tells me lies, and that none of the things that it reports ever happened. I have no senses. Body, shape, extensions, movement and place are chimeras. So what remains true? Perhaps just the one fact that nothing is certain." (Descartes 1996, II, 24)

Latter Descartes comes to the conclusion that at least his existence is true. The sentence "*I am, I exist* is necessarily true whenever it is put forward by me or conceived in my mind." (Descartes, II, 25) If it were not, doubting ones existence would not be possible, nor would it be possible for a "deceiver of supreme power" to deceive that one is a mental substance and that God exists – a fact that makes cognition about cognition and self-awareness possible in the first place. A certain fact is something that is evident and that does not depend on our senses (senses can mislead us). For something to be evident, an idea should be presented to us clear and distinct.

As an opponent of rationalism, postmodernism does not strive to find the criterion to "find" reality, but simply acknowledges that nothing is real and that everything is an impression or an illusion.

Unspeakable truth or the revelation of truth on the face of the Other

Despite of all, postmodern thought is not that radical. It does not abolish the notion of truth completely. Postmodern thought sees truth as inexpressible, unreachable, as something that is beyond our being. But if human being is thrown into existence, compassion reveals itself in the limitations of beings, that we face, as a possibility to understand the existentials of fear and terror. Being is therefore being(-there) with others. It demands a compassionate relationship.

Let us turn to the question of truth. Prior to post-structuralism, which is known for its focus on the question of difference or "différance" (Jacques Derrida, Gilles Deleuze), Emmanuel Levinas used the notion of difference when discussing the Other. He was describing the face as a way to "get to the truth", a truth that is beyond our reality. Truth, he says, is revealed on the face of the Other.

In *Time and the Other* Levinas talks about the existence of a difference, a difference in the absolute sense, a difference where the distinction (of opposing parts in a relation) is not being diminished by the relationship between itself and its counterpart: a difference that allows each part to remain absolutely different. This difference is the feminine. "What is the alterity that does not purely and simply enter into the opposition of two species of the same genus? I think the absolutely contrary contrary [*le contraire absolutement contraire*], whose contrariety is in no way affected by the relationship that can be established between it and its correlative, the contrariety that permits its terms to remain absolutely other, is feminine." (Levinas 1997, 85)

Levinas introduced the concept of the feminine, the different, before he spoke about the concept of the face. The feminine is more than just a distinction between genders, more than a grammatical difference between the masculine and the feminine gender, and more than just a logical distinction. This difference signifies pure transcendence emerging from the concept of the feminine. It is the situation where the alterity of the other is being given in its purest form. (Levinas 1997, 85)

The feminine for Levinas is something fundamentally different. This difference is not meant in a romantic sense. The feminine in existence is an event, not like an event of special transcendence; the feminine is "a flight before light." (Levinas 1997, 87) The feminine is an ability to accept the absolute different. It is not the activity of opposition, but the ability of pure passiveness. The feminine is being available to the Other. That is why the feminine is hospitality, and hospitality carries within the ability to accept the pure alterity of the Other and to accept truth, that cannot be encapsulated with words. The feminine is a turning point in Levinas's thought: at first it signifies the pure difference and the pure otherness, which leads to the concept of the face, a concept Levinas develops further after *Time and the Other.* Once he comes to the notion of the face, the feminine becomes "me". The face becomes the precondition in order to become the feminine, to be able to accept the transcendence, the totality of the Other.

Compassion and the Face

It is the horizon of the feminine where we want to ask the question: What is the face in Levinas' thought? Levinas` concept of the face is influenced by Husserl's phenomenology, which means that he describes humans based on the perceived essence that emerges before him, although Levinas is cautious when he talks about the phenomenology of the face, because phenomenology describes what appears. (Levinas 1998, 57) In his own words, Levinas states that the best way to encounter the Other is to "not even notice the colour of his eyes." (Levinas 1998, 57) The face, he says, cannot be reduced to its appearance. "The first thing we notice is the immediacy of the face, its nudity and defenselessness. The face is the part of the body that is usually not covered, it is exposed ..." (Levinas 1998, 57)

The *face is exposed*, menaced, as if inviting us to an act of violence (Levinas 1998, 57) It is, however, in this frailty and exposure, in this weakness that we discover a new shade of its essence (the essence of the face): the moral power of the face. The lack of physical power is its ethical power. The more exposed it is, the more powerful is the ethical imperative, which is saying "Do not kill, do not kill me!" In other words, the face is saying "do not injure me", "do not hurt me", "do not disappoint me" and "help me."

The demand of ethics is a call to sacredness. "No one can say: 'I've done all that was asked of me ...' This reveals openness for what is beyond our limitations. That is the presence of Infinity." (Levinas 1998, 69).

In the face-to-face relation with the Other a trace of the infinite is being revealed. Infinity is not just suffering, distress or despair, but also a call for help (a call to me for help).

In this context, Levinas speaks of listening in two senses:

1. To hear the actual words asking for help, to hear a sigh; and
2. Ethical listening, being open (not just listening and to listen, but to hear and respond to the call of the Other).

Compassion, which emerges from the ethical significance of listening (listening and accepting the Other), is accepting the truth that is shown on the face of the Other. This truth includes responsibility (for the Other). But Levinas was not an advocate of compassion (*com-passion*). In fact, in his later works he revoked the term, because he feared that his ethics could be understood as a feeling or an emotional relationship with the other. Emotions can vary, they change, but ethical responsibility cannot, and should not be the result of emotions, but of the human intellect. It is like a demand of common sense, it is an imperative. "We are all responsible for everyone else - but I am more responsible than all the others" - a remark that is spoken by Alyosha Karamazov in The Brothers Karamazov, is one that Levinas is fond of quoting. Its challenge is an excessive one: a mode of being and saying where I am endlessly obligated to the Other, a multiplicity in being which refuses totalization and takes form instead as fraternity and discourse, an ethical relation which forever precedes and exceeds the egoism and tyranny of ontology (Hand 1989, 1).

Levinas argued that compassion in the context of ethics could only be the highest form of human intellect that transcends the revelation of being-there through thought. Compassion is "listening to being", listening beyond truth. At the same time, however, listening is a clear and conceptual revelation that emerges out from the call, that is coming from the face (of the Other) in front of me.

We could conclude that Levinas' ethics describes a new approach in metaphysics. The center of his metaphysics is not ontology, but rather ethical responsibility. For Levinas truth and reality are not matters of epistemology (a method to get closer to the truth) first, but questions of ethics. Levinas' ethical responsibility for the Other (the face) is not an emotional and intuitive response, nor it is a form of emotional intelligence. Truth (is something that) speaks to me. The truth that is revealed on the face of the Other excites me, awakens my compassion for the Other and makes me sensible for the Other.

We could add that the excitement, the feeling of being absorbed by the Other, exposes compassion (passion) for the Other. Compassion is not something emerging within me, it is revealed - revealed from the Other. Compassion is not an emotion, but something intelligible, a new reasoning, that guides me towards the Other and empowers me to do something for the Other. This is the transition from compassion to responsibility. That is why we can argue that Levinas' ethic is a response on the level of speaking and language. Compassion is an intellectual, ethical discourse that calls on me to act. The face, which reveals infinity, demands endless responsibility, because its call for me to act never stops.

Conclusion

Levinas' notion of truth is the truth that reveals itself in a response, or in the traces of infinity on the face of the Other. In order to accept and understand this truth (and with it the transcendence, the totality of the Other), one must "become" pure feminine, that is, become pure availability, which listens to truth and lets it guide oneself into the past, which is gone and beyond its reach, and into the future, which is already here. It reveals the totality of the Other and truth in the purest form. This notion of truth is a difficult concept to grasp and understand, but it can be lived. My responsibility for the Other (or towards the Other) outruns the Other's wishes or his pleas for help and that is why answering this call is never finished and has no end.

References

Benn, P. 2006. *Ethics: Fundamentals of Philosophy*. London and New York: Routledge.

Descartes, R. 1996. *Meditations on First Philosophy*. Transl. by John Cottingham. Cambridge: Cambridge University Press.

Hand, S. 1989. *The Levinas reader*. Oxford: Basil Blackwell.

Jamnik, A. 1998. *Liberalizem in vprašanje etike*. Ljubljana: Nova revija.

Juhant, J. 1993. Človek, temelj etike? *Bogoslovni vestnik* 53: 125–134.

Kos, J. 1995. *Na poti v postmoderno*. Ljubljana: Literarno- umetniško društvo Literatura.

Levinas, E. 1998. *Etika in neskončno. Čas in drugi*. Ljubljana: Družina.

Levinas, E. 1997. *Time and the Other*. Transl. by Richard A. Cohen. Seventh Printing. Pittsburgh, Pennsylvania: Duquesne University Press.

MacNiven, D. 2005. *Creative Morality*. London and New York: Routlege, 2005.

Senegačnik, B. 1998. *V iskanju izgubljene mere*. Ljubljana: Študentska založba.

Sorč, C. 1999. Teologija kot ubesedovanje Molka, Intervju s teologom Brunom Fortejem. *Tretji dan*, XXVIII (254/255): 16.

COMPASSION AS A WAY OF LIVING THE TRUTH

Erika Prijatelj, Ljubljana

1. Introduction

The premise of this paper is that truth and compassion are interconnected. We argue that truth cannot be known without compassion. Compassion is like a door, which needs to be opened in order to get closer to the truth. To support this position, we will first analyze two different concepts of the truth, Greek and Hebraic, and subsequently verify their possible application toward an understanding of compassion. Assisted by various authors, such as Taylor, Reilly, Schopenhauer and the Dalai Lama, we will attempt to define and explain the notion of compassion. We advocate the view that it is necessary to develop compassion both at the individual and societal level in order that truth emerges under the form of interpersonal and societal justice, a justice that goes beyond a legalistic view of the person.

2. Two different concepts of truth: Greek and Hebraic

The Greek word for truth is ALETHEIA. The Greeks understood that word to mean something that is not hidden, not masked, not in a state of concealment and as such something that is in a state of clarity and evident. This approach supports the view that truth is always present, open and accessible to all; thus, nothing remains camouflaged and unclear. We are tasked to remove everything that separates us from the truth or that, which prevents us to be in touch not with that, which is merely accidental but with that, which is real and essential regarding our nature.

According to Plato truth is a static property, which leads to metaphysical speculation about the essences and the universals as something more real than that, which encompasses the everyday world. Despite efforts to know the truth and the good only a few ever reach such a level that they are able to express something meaningful about these universals and even that expression itself remains limited to a symbolic level. Although Socrates admits that he does not know what the good is, however, he is willing to share with his students the fruits of the good (Plato 1992, 506). Complete understanding of the truth thus remains the privilege of the gods. It is the task of people to remain in constant quest to disclose the truth by "trying to "awaken the best part of the soul and lead it upward to the study of the best among the things that are …" (Plato 1992, 532).

The Hebraic concept of truth, EMET, does not deny the importance of the Greek view, which emphasis the harmony between the particular and the universal. However, EMET offers a focus, which is more dynamic, changeable and embracing. This does not mean that the Hebraic understanding of truth is in constant flux. This Hebraic concept also implies strength, stability and duration. As it involves the formation of human nature and the restoration of the world, truth is dynamic.

The Hebraic view is grounded in the belief that God created the whole of reality, including the reality of *doing*. Having been created by God, it is our responsibility to complete the work of God's creation. Consequently, whenever a person makes a decision that person must also be aware that an account of his/her decision must be rendered to God. (Armesto 1997, 77–78) The truth is therefore not only a question of "to be", but also a question of "to act". Being real means to be with the truth, to live in the truth or even more importantly to be a part of the truth. Truth can be likened to a spirit; it is like a fire that inspires and shapes our decisions from within. Truth is embodied in people who follow it in their endeavors. No place, no experience nor is any person exempted from the presence of truth. People who are in touch with the truth experience solidity and stability in their life. The truth is neither objective nor static; it is not something that could be studied from a distance. The truth is very close. It is a personal way of living, a way of being and, therefore, very relational.

Which view is more adequate, at this point, is an understandable query. In this paper, we take the position that it is not a question regarding which notion of truth is better: Greek or Hebraic. We propose the view that it is necessary to consider both concepts of truth, which will be supported with additional clarification in connection with our understanding of compassion.

3. Compassion in Oliner's story

Charles Taylor related the story of Samuel and Pearl Oliner. Because they rescued many Jews during the Nazi's persecution, the couple Oliner was honored as "righteous gentiles", an appellation to which they totally objected.

"We are now called Righteous Gentiles or even sometimes heroes. We much object to this title and I can tell you why. One day there was an air raid on the German barracks near our house, some five kilometres away. My husband happened to be there. When it was over, the barracks were badly hit. A German soldier came running out with his head practically destroyed. He was bleeding heavily and obviously in shock. He was running in panic.

My husband saw that within minutes he would fall down and bleed to death. So my husband put him on his bicycle – without thinking about it – and brought him to the commandant's house. He put him on the step, rang the bell, waited to see the door open and left. Later some of our friends and people who were hiding with us heard about it and said: 'You are a traitor because you helped the enemy.' My husband replied: 'No, the moment the man was badly wounded, he was not an enemy any more but simply a human being in need.' As little as we would accept the title of traitor, so little can we accept the title of hero for the things we did to help to Jewish people. We just helped human beings who were in need" (Taylor 1999, 74-75).

Compassion denotes one who is "suffering with" another person who suffers. Viewing compassion in this way, we can understand Charles Taylor's articulation of compassion as a "primitive response" and that which we clearly witnessed in the deeds of Samuel and Pearl Oliner. One is compassionate to the extent that one has the capacity to suffer with others. Therefore, a compassionate person is able to feel concern for the overall good of others and motivated to engage appropriate and helpful actions for their sake. However, a compassionate response is not toward another's pain *per se* but toward a person who suffers unnecessarily. At times, some pain is necessary for one's personal growth (Reilly 2008, 33). For example, children do not need to be overprotected nor sheltered from all pain, as this type of caretaking would not show an appropriate concern for a child's healthy development and individualization. It is also this paper's position, which does not endorse a definition of compassionate acts simply as acts that alleviate another's suffering and pain.

As we witnessed in the example of the couple Oliner, compassion is greater and nobler than pity. "Pity has its roots in fear and carries a sense of arrogance and condescension, sometimes even a smug feeling of 'I'm glad it's not me'" (Reilly 2008, 21). As Stephen Levine says: "When your fear touches someone's pain, it becomes pity, when your love touches someone's pain, it becomes compassion" (Levine 2012, 68).

Taylor characterizes compassion as a "primitive response" to the suffering of the other (Taylor 1999, 86). By primitive response he means that when a person assists the suffering other this action is not mediated by reason or even thought that the other's suffering is a good reason to act. Rather it is "its spontaneity and it expresses a constitutive element of our human nature" (Reilly 2008, 22). The response is primitive also in the sense that it cannot be explained empirically in terms of more fundamental categories or facts about people. In this way, compassion is a bedrock for truly moral conduct similar to Arthur Schopenhauer's views on compassion. According to Schopenhauer compassion is "the immediate participation, independent of all ulterior consideration, primarily in the suffering of another and thus in the prevention or elimination of it; for all satisfaction and well-being consists in this. It is simply and solely this compassion that is the real basis for all voluntary justice and genuine loving-kindness. Only insofar as an action has sprung from compassion does it have moral value" (Schopenhauer 1995, 144).

On some occasions, most people show compassion naturally or spontaneously. On one hand, this fact supports both Taylor's claim that compassion is a "primitive response" that characterizes human nature and Schopenhauer's assertion that compassion is an "everyday phenomenon" (Schopenhauer 1995, 138). Many people intend or aspire to act compassionately toward others always when there is a need for it. By such actions they broaden and deepen their compassionate responsiveness to people's suffering. On the other hand, some people intentionally act with a purpose of not protecting or not saving people from unnecessary suffering or they may even cause suffering. For people who want to act compassionately such deficiencies or evil behavior stand out as a lack of moral responsibility.

According to Reilly who follows Schopenhauer's lead, the "ethics of compassion are grounded in one's mindful commitment to one's own happiness with the recognition that the well being that one wishes for oneself is likewise wished by others. Indeed, it is one's commitment to the well being of others as well as oneself that best assures a life of joy and contentment." (Reilly 2008, 1). Schopenhauer argued that *Mitleid,*[1] a desire for another's well-being, is possible only if another's misery directly becomes the same sort of motivation as our own misery. Just as painful experiences contrary to our will move us in ways to relieve them, by having compassion toward another, another's misery assumes the same status as our own by moving us to relieve it.

4. Buddhism's view of compassion

Buddhism originates in the teachings of Shakyamuni (Gautama Siddartha), who lived some 2,500 years ago in India. When the teacher Shakyamuni Buddha first spoke about the Dharma he taught the *four noble truths*: the truth of suffering, the cause of suffering, the cessation of suffering and the path to the cessation of suffering. Based on these truths, among world religions Buddhism remains the most concerned with the issue of compassion. The Dalai Lama, a prominent representative of Tibetan Buddhism, says that such an interest in the inner value of compassion as we find it in the West has not been met anywhere else in the

1 Schopenhauer's Mitleid (Compassion) is not Nietzsche's Mitleid (Pity).

world. One might ask why the West and not in India or Senegal? Responding to this query the Dalai Lama explains (Dalai Lama 2001, 8): "Because [in the West] as far as material comfort is concerned, this is already achieved, yet people are not happy. So now, through their own experience, people are looking for an alternative."

In accordance with the Dalai Lama, we propose that the greatest degree of inner peace emanates from the development of love and compassion. The more we care for the happiness of others, the more we experience our own sense of well-being. Cultivating a close, warm-hearted feeling for others simultaneously puts our mind at ease. This helps to remove fears or insecurities we may have and gives us the strength to cope with obstacles we encounter. Developing love and compassion is the ultimate source of success in life. When we recognize that we are all equal, both in our desire for happiness and in our right to obtain it, we are able to feel empathy for and closeness to others. (5-7)

The Dalai Lama defines true compassion as "not just an emotional response but a firm commitment founded on reason. Therefore, a truly compassionate attitude towards others does not change even if they behave negatively" (10). This statement is an admission by the Dalai Lama that true compassion is not easy to achieve. We can experience it only when we eliminate self-centeredness and our deep attachment to the feeling of independence. As stated by the Dalai Lama "the most significant obstacles to compassion are anger and hatred" (11). These are extremely powerful emotions and they can overwhelm our entire mind.

It is the Dalai Lama's firm belief that compassion or loving-kindness develops through training and reasoning; it does not grow spontaneously. The Dalai Lama makes a distinction between emotions and compassion. He emphasizes that emotions are given to us by nature and are part of us; they do not need to be cultivated. Nature is a good starting point. However, nature "provides" compassion focused on "our people", such as our immediate family. If we wish to direct compassion toward all people, we need to cultivate this value. (Ekman 2008, 140-141) For instance, we do not need to learn how to be angry but we do need to learn how to be compassionately angry. Furthermore, we need to learn how to be compassionate with those who are not compassionate with us.

Loving-kindness, as discussed above, is understood in Buddhist literature in two different ways. One way focuses on the suffering of the other, on the wish to see the other free from suffering. In this regard, loving-kindness is the wish that the other attains happiness. However, for the practice of compassion the other way of loving-kindness is seen as even more important. It is translated as "connectedness, a sense of endearment to others, where the idea is cultivating a state of mind that makes the sight of other's suffering unbearable to you" (163).

The stronger this sense of connectedness is part of us, the stronger our feeling of unbearableness will be, when we see the other suffer.

In line with Buddhist tradition, compassion is both a rational and an emotional response to suffering. Furthermore, it is also the Dalai Lama's view that compassion includes "the wish that all sentient beings be free of suffering" (Dalai Lama 2001, 96). This position presumes that this wish is ardent and active. As the Dalai Lama states: "True compassion has the intensity and spontaneity of a loving mother caring for her suffering baby." (105) Therefore, a compassionate person both suffers and struggles with people who suffer. This view also echoes the writings of Augustine and Aquinas regarding mercy: "As Augustine says … *mercy is heartfelt sympathy for another's distress, impelling us to succor him if we can.* For mercy takes its name misericordia from denoting a man's compassionate heart (miserum cor), at the sight of another's unhappiness" (Aquinas 1920, Q. 30, Art. 1).

5. Compassion at the collective level

Compassion needs to be demonstrated both at the individual and collective levels. Even though a personal experience of compassion is absolutely necessary, compassion only on the individual level is not sufficient. The level of moral healthiness of one community, society or nation is evidenced by the pervasiveness and intensity of societal compassion. Societal compassion based on a personal practice of compassion is a path toward justice. In this context, we understand justice, which is grounded in compassion as a value, which far surpasses a term legalistic justice. Compassionate justice is a concrete expression of truth; it is truth with both its static and dynamic dimension.

As stated by Melvin James (James 2009, 324-327) a compassionate society is characterized by the following criteria. It has a strong belief in the intrinsic value and dignity of every person regardless of his/her political, economic, social and religious condition. It also has a systemic comprehension of the economic, social, religious and political factors that contribute to people becoming oppressed, destitute, marginalized or poor in the society. This means that a society needs to be other–centered and that in the process of ongoing materialism and individualism we do not become emotionally fossilized. A compassionate society is a humanitarian society where the Golden Rule is incorporated in all facets of society. The Golden Rule: "Do unto others as we would have others do unto us", can be transformed into a Compassionate Rule, when we can say: "The quality of life you desire for yourself, should guide you in creating the quality of life for others" (James 2009, 326).

Based on these characteristics of a compassionate society two levels of compassionate responsibility can be established. The first level demonstrates personal responsibility rooted in each person to be compassionate to those in need. The second level demonstrates compassion at the institutional level. To support this society needs an institutional compassionate leadership, which cares for those who struggle and suffer.

Every society has a choice either to facilitate a path of truth and compassion or a path of falsehoods and meanness. Truth promotes justice and compassion promotes peace. When truth and compassion work together, there is a pathway toward justice and peace; where truth and compassion do not work together, the pathway leads to injustice and violence.

6. Conclusion

Compassion, like the truth, has both a static and a dynamic dimension. It is simply not enough to make a singular discovery regarding the importance of the value of compassion; rather regular, repeated practice is necessary in our daily life if we wish to rediscover and deepen our understanding of it. Respect and compassion for others does not automatically occur; a strong personal commitment and exercise is required. "To train in compassion is to know that all people are the same and suffer in similar ways to honor those who suffer and to know that we are neither separate from nor superior to anyone" (Rinpoche 2012, 59).

Moreover, compassion is not one-sided. Due to its relational character, it is a dynamic interactive process. This means both are enriched: those who show compassion toward those who suffer, as well as those who endure suffering. Our personal and societal identity is in an ongoing process of being reshaped because of the dynamism of compassion. The manner by which we enter into relationship with others is at the same time the manner in which we reveal ourselves.

When we are faced with a dilemma regarding which to choose: truth or compassion, a static or dynamic perspective, a personal or societal level of responsibility, etc., we confront the limits of dualistic thinking. Such thinking traps us on a rational argumentative level. Consequently, this implies that one manner of thinking is right and another manner of thinking is wrong. An alternative way to seek truth is through compassion. Taking this approach, we do not assume that we possess the truth. Rather we open ourselves to new aspects of the truth and in this way, we self-transcend. Compassion is therefore a qualitatively new approach toward discovering truth. In fact, with daily practice it becomes a way of living the truth.

References

Aquinas, T. 1920. *Summa Theologica.* Trans. by Fathers of the English Dominican Province. London: Burns, Oates & Washbourne, Ltd.

Armesto, F. F. 1997. *TRUTH. A History and a Guide for the Perplexed.* New York, NY: St. Martin's Press.

Dalai Lama. 2001. *An Open Heart: Practicing Compassion in Everyday Life.* Boston, MA: Nicholas Vreeland (ed.), Little Brown and Company.

Dalai Lama. 2012. *Compassion and the Individual,* Mountain View, CA: Dharamsala, Library of Tibetan Works & Archives.

Ekman, P. 2008. *Emotional Awareness – Overcoming the Obstacles to Psychological Balance (A Conversation between the Dalai Lama and Paul Ekman).* New York, NY: Times Books.

James, M. 2009. *Contemporary Analyses of Truth, Justice, and Compassion.* New York, NY: Create Space.

Levine, S. 2012. *Who Dies? An Investigation of Conscious Living and Conscious Dying.* New York, NY: Anchor Books.

Plato. 1992. *Republic.* Trans. by G.M.A. Grube. Indianapolis: Hackett Publishing Company.

Reilly, R. 2008. *Ethics of Compassion. Bridging Ethical Theory and Religious Moral.* New York, NY: Lexington Books.

Rinpoche, S. 2012. *The Tibetan Book of Living and Dying: 20th Anniversary,* London, UK: Harper One.

Schopenhauer, A. 1995. *On the Basis of Morality.* Cambridge, UK: Hacket Publishing Company.

Taylor, Ch. 1999. Sympathy. *The Journal of Ethics,* 2(3): 73-78.

CHRISTIAN-SPIRITUAL WAY OUT OF ANTHROPOLOGICAL COMPASSION TRAP

Marcin Godawa, Krakow

In human life, it may happen that such a noble value as compassion is abused right up to forming *a compassion trap* by separating it from the whole truth about life. Thus, fed with emotions, man is unable to recognize where the real solution to his or her problems lies. Starting with the description of the situation and according to the methodology of spiritual theology, the rescuing role of the grace of God will be exposed in the next two points, namely the stirring function of grace – as an effective and gentle way out – will be confirmed by a selected example. Sources cited here, of high or even the highest authority, underline the meaning of the Catholic message to man.

1. Trap – compassion away from whole truth

The term "compassion" occurs here in the sense of sharing somebody's emotions, mainly painful as it is used in the English field of psychology (Reber 2002). Facing one's situation is consequently and frequently connected with a wish to offer some help to him or her in the name of humanity. In general, such a very positive attitude joins secular beliefs of modern humanism (Camus) with the Catholic Church's teaching and practice. St. Paul's appeal: "Rejoice with those who rejoice, weep with those who weep. Have the same regard one for another" (Rom 12:15-16)'[1] shows us that the ability to empathize and show compassion pertains to Christian identity, to the building up social life and ultimately to the order of God's salvation (Salij 1986, 12–14). Undoubtedly, compassion as a kind of higher emotions, can and very often does play the very important role in making life better so that it is unimaginable to think of human life without it.

However, among anthropological questions, genuine compassion may become an impediment to human development and that is why it is here rendered by the word *a trap*. The problem lies in *separating* compassion from the main core of life when one is so absorbed with showing his or her empathy that he omits to look for a real solution to other's situation. Compassion arises as an overstressed

1 The Biblical quotations derived from the *New American Bible*.

quality that involves human capacities, the quality of sense destroyed because a sense means relating something to some appropriate wholeness whereas compassion is here split off from its broader context. The question is even sharpened in contemporary times when man has stopped deriving the sense of moral life from God and from the nature. Having rejected the idea of general sense of life, man tries to articulate himself more through self-epiphany in order to acknowledge the existence of humanistic values (Taylor 2012). In this context, the compassion trap makes a most distinct point of reference for research though at times situations of a *possible* trap are considered.

The question of compassion trap will be undertaken here in terms of the Catholic Church's spiritual theology to show her logical and coherent interpretation of human life to which she has still the right and which is worthy of the attention of non-believers too. However, the teaching embraces plenty of cases of moral and physical evil, which is best to consider as a sin for the sake of clarity. Today it is very popular and politically correct to express deep compassion to homosexual persons, especially when reportedly persecuted. Leaving aside some social questions, compassion for them tends to understand their situation with its hardships. As long as being connected with the whole Church's view, such a kind of empathy remains a form of actual care for a neighbor, far from acceptance of his or her sin. But the moment of disconnection entails dysfunction while one's whole care is directed to empathy but not to search for a way out. This is the point of distinguishing compassion from mercy, as Tischner holds it (Tischner 1999, 13–23). A sinner may be bestowed with an enhanced emotional attitude insofar that he or she fails to perceive and receive real help. Feeling sorry for a sick person accompanied by no attempt to give him or her medicine or confining the treatment to measuring only body temperature illustrates the problem. Above all, compassion goes against truth or more exactly, it opposes the whole truth about man's life. It is interesting that this process of rescission of truth reaches out to the matter of language when a word "sin" or "evil" is denied with emotionality far away from objectiveness but using a category of hateful speech.

Meanwhile, the Church's response remains fully opened to truth, on the one hand to empathically understand man embroiled in sin, while on the other hand to evoke the whole truth about his or her life. The crucial step is to bring a sinner back to the main core of his life, as it has been revealed by God. In the light of divine infinite love which "rejoices with the truth" (1 Cor 13:6) a sinner starts to see both the right prospect for him and proper means given to achieve that goal. Following the call coming from the whole truth, he or she is enabled to resolve the problem effectively. Then, by referring to the fullness of truth, the sense of compassion is restored anew.

2. Grace of God – gentle and effective way out

In this context, the Church's answer is summoned up with the word *grace* along with a proper explanation, as it follows:

Grace is, first and foremost the gift of the Spirit who justifies and sanctifies us. But grace also includes the gifts that the Spirit grants us to associate us with his work, to enable us to collaborate in the salvation of others and in the growth of the Body of Christ, the Church (*Catechism* 2015, 2003).

The idea of God's free gift means that grace is originally produced by God and cannot be gained by any man's effort (*Catechism* 2015, 2010). That is why man is not the author of final happiness and that he or she needs God's grace as a necessary condition of salvation. With respect to the present consideration, it is grace that brings a sinner back to the whole truth about life. This effect is achieved mainly through the sanctifying grace which "makes us 'pleasing to God'" (*Catechism* 2015, 2014) by erasing sins and making the bond of love, called the divine "adoption" of man by God (Rom 8:14-21). Thus, the *personal* character of grace must be strongly stressed so that the gift of grace is simply "God alone communicating himself to man, so to speak God pouring himself into a human soul" (Wojtyła 1987, 1241). Such a grace-relation is always an interpersonal event where each of Three God's Persons affects human personality. While the word "gift" - renders the Redeemer's initiative role and His free attitude towards humans - then the word "collaboration" points out that man is stirred to give his or her free answer.

However, grace ascribed with "the gifts" also embraces - along with its sanctifying effect - plenty of particular questions of that cooperation. In the end, the gift(s) of grace suggest(s) that every necessary means of curing is granted to a sinner. Saint Cyril of Jerusalem explains it by connotations of water applied to the Holy Spirit. The picture of the rain which "while remaining essentially the same, it adapts itself to the needs of every creature that receives it" displays the acting Spirit who "simple and indivisible, apportions grace to each man as he wills" (Cyril 2015). The clear meaningful relevance ought to be expounded as follows: the Spirit *adapts* himself to each of man's needs and grants him or her each of particular required gifts. Thus, this is God alone who can effectively bring man out of the compassion trap.

When a neighbor's unprofitable sympathy gives way to the divine power then a sinner is being treated by the most excellent, deepest and saving *compassion* of the Ghost. Such a term may convey what St. Cyril puts:

"The Spirit comes gently and makes himself known by his fragrance. He is not felt as a burden, for he is light, very light. Rays of light and knowledge stream before him as he approaches. The Spirit comes with the tenderness of a true friend and protector to save, to heal, to teach, to counsel, to strengthen, to console" (Cyril 2015).

A set of terms that is "gently", "fragrance", "light", "tenderness", "a true friend and protector" along with the verbs describing His action among which there is also "to console", mean that just here the true and full compassion for man arises. Wishes for being snuggled as well as emotional needs are actually fulfilled so that man ought to be sure to be both effectively and gently treated. Being stuck in the compassion trap can be successfully replaced with spiritual transmutation including knowledge ("to teach"), emotions ("to console") and will (the aforementioned "to collaborate") but aiming at salvation ("to save").

The three terms: *freedom*, *gentleness* and *effectiveness* which characterize the cooperation of man with grace may be further explained by so called *Indiculus* (ca. 440) which represents the common Church doctrine, still valid. Firstly, God is confessed to be "the author of all good dispositions of mind, and also of works, and of all zeal, and of all virtues". Consequently, His grace is the first and necessary principle of human doing: "all the merits of man are preceded by His grace", yet that does not harm human freedom: "free choice is not taken away by this aid and gift of God, but it is set at liberty". As referred to God and by virtue of His goodness people have been called to share God's merits as their own and they gain the status of "cooperators with the grace of God" (*Indiculus* [1], 141).

Within the present text, also the question of *how* the grace works in man can be interestingly answered. The authors says of God: "He acts in us that we may both will and do what He wishes" (*Indiculus* [1], 141). The grace agitates a soul embracing both human will and acts or in other words potential and actual dimensions of life. Thence, the grace is necessary not only to make sins forgiven (*Indiculus* [1], 136) or to let somebody know the commandments (137) but also to be a spur for willing and doing. This truth - belonging to the heart of the issue - is conveyed by similar formulas, that is "the power" granted "to love and to be able to do that which we know to be ought to be done" (*Indiculus* [1], 137) or in the original Latin text: "etiam facere diligamus atque valeamus" (*Indiculus* [2], 245). From both of them the meaning of being endowed with power and love in order to act, clearly derives. It has previously been acknowledged that "in each and every good movement of the human will, His help is more powerful" or in Latin: "in bonis quibusque voluntatis humanae singulis motibus magis illius valere, non dubitemus, auxilium" (*Indiculus* [2], 243). Thus, the grace is the first agent which dominates over human life and being freely participated by man grants its own power to man, stirs him or her and supplies effectiveness to the process of collaboration. This is the way in which getting out of the compassion trap is carried out. What is impossible for pure human sympathy when separated from the whole truth, that becomes actual by external intervention while the main burden of liberation process is borne by God. The grace is proclaimed to be such an answer which *attracts* man - the word *grace* (Gr. χάρις, *charis*] indeed means something very kind, pleasant and enjoyable (Abramowiczówna 1965) - if only prejudices are removed. In terms of emotions the human need for being snuggled and quiet is successfully responded (cf. Rom 15:7). Even if some hardships continue they are prompted by human weakness not by the grace-prospect of which there is no real reason to cherish any fear.

In view of gaining better understanding of the presentation of grace as the agent, bringing man back to the whole truth must be shown in its entirety. It is necessary to point out that eschatology makes the principle which determines perceiving the process of leaving the trap of compassion for what is divine, which could be put in the following scheme:

a. human life along with its needs terminates at heaven only in which "every tear" will be wiped by God and where shall be "no more death or mourning, wailing or pain" (Rev. 21:4). Therefore *a new heaven* (Rev. 21;1) could be named the final point of compassing work of grace;
b. according to that ultimate truth each of the human hardships within the temporal life must be participated in the work of grace to be carried to the happy fulfilment. However, at that point practical life diverges into two dimensions:
   b1. for the situations which could be healed - like managing spiritual crisis or forgiving sins - the scope ought to be achieved as much as possible;
   b2. for the rest which cannot be healed in this life - like some kinds of suffering - man should allow the grace to work in his or her life to enjoy its effects described by Jesus as "my yoke is easy, and my burden light" (Mt 11:30).

Since this is grace, which brings man right up to the final happiness, then the first and main condition is to be united with her and that is why purification from mortal sins - which break the bond of grace - means the crucial step to be taken. As long as man offers help by showing emotions provided that he, being in the state of grace, he or she is on the way to the final curing. Here the very wide room for human compassion is made because - as related to the whole truth about human life - it could be now fruitfully applied. Only if having participated in the *process* of cooperation with grace the worth of human empathy is implemented and fully revealed.

3. From compassion to truth – St. Augustine's example

The question of grace which brings man out of (potentially)[2] helpless compassion to the whole and saving truth, may be followed by the analysis of St. Augustine's auto-description of spiritual breakthrough put in his *Confessions*. The author entertains himself as a person going through deep spiritual crisis, focused on feeling his own misery and on the desire for the truth that means God alone in terms of a personal relationship with Him. The crisis consists in strong emotional bursting provoked by meditation and rendered by the formula: "a mighty storm, accompanied by a mighty rain of tears" or by repetitive cry: "And thou, O Lord, how long? How long, O Lord? Wilt thou be angry forever? Oh, remember not against us our former iniquities" (Augustine 2015, VIII. 12). Alypius, Augustine's cordial friend, representing compassionate attitude, is still present there but this is his assistance that is intentionally pushed away by Augustine, on account of being inadequate and helpless to the situation from which he suffers so much:

"I stole away from Alypius, for it seemed to me that solitude was more appropriate for the business of weeping. I went far enough away that I could feel that even his presence was no restraint upon me" (Augustine 2015, VIII.12).

It becomes to be clear that Alypius' empathy is limited and that man cannot reach out to the heart of the other's problem. Here the compassion cannot supply any effective support to the struggle and the friend accepts it: "This was the way I felt at the time, and he realized it." Just at this point, when remaining in his *passive* distance, he avoids making his compassion a trap whereas the right moment for his aid will come.

The solution comes from outside the relationship between Alypius and Augustine as well as his own inner world. The vehicle of this help is a voice singing: "Pick it up, read it; pick it up, read it" (*Tolle, lege; tolle, lege*) whose mysterious character is testified by the fact that the voice sounds beyond ordinary compassion in the sense of sharing somebody's mood only because it signifies a step forward, diverting attention from the circle of sorrow[3].

Consequently, this interference results in ceased weeping and in such a reaction:

2 *Nota bene*, this situation could have become a compassion trap; however, such a case was avoided.

3 The outer genesis of the voice is marked also by the fact that Augustine cannot recognize from what kind of play it may come.

"[...] damming the torrent of my tears, I got to my feet, for I could not but think that this was a divine command to open the Bible and read the first passage I should light upon" (Augustine 2015, VIII. 12.).

The step forward is marked by standing firmly, ("I got to my feet") which along with damming the tears, reflects the recapture of personal power but the most important thing is the religious and spiritual character of the breakthrough. The voice has been interpreted by Augustine unambiguously as "a divine command" to read the first biblical passage he would meet[4]. Indeed, the words about turning to Christ (Rom 13:13) [5] bring him the appropriate aid displayed as follows: "there was infused in my heart something like the light of full certainty and all the gloom of doubt vanished away". The *certainty* of his experience signifies the solution of the problem of which quickness against the non-surmountable depth of previous crisis stresses the power of grace. After all, the voice represents the grace of God named directly "a divine command". At this point, the idea of cooperation appears since the grace is said to spur man to go forward while man is claimed to follow the grace freely. Exploring the question, one can notice that the emerging grace is being received through human *interpretation* - just like Augustine perceived the voice as "a divine command" to pick up the Bible - and that the veracity of such an association is justified by results, here by the peaceful certainty which Augustine had needed.

The intentional following grace delivers man out of the limited empathy or a (possible) trap of compassion to the whole truth about life evoked here by the feature of certainty. All this can be illustrated by the sequence of Augustine's movement: lying down – getting to his feet – going to the place where the Bible was left – coming up to Alypius – and to Monica, his mother. In the end their *stand-by-role* is revealed too. Alypius - strengthened by next words out of the same passage - becomes finally able to share Augustine's state ("he joined me in full commitment without any restless hesitation") which means that his presence is being activated by following the act of grace. Similarly, it is time to show Monica's feelings to her son. In general, the scene expounds compassion as an important value limited but also fruitful when it takes its proper place in the fundamental guidance of the grace of God.

4 The method supported by St. Antonius' example.

5 "Not in rioting and drunkenness, not in chambering and wantonness, not in strife and envying, but put on the Lord Jesus Christ, and make no provision for the flesh to fulfill the lusts thereof" [Augustine 2015, VIII.12].

Conclusion

The presentation may be summoned up in a few statements:

- the compassion trap is produced by separating empathy from the whole truth about man;
- the truth is expressed by the grace of God, which means the gentle and effective solution to such a problem;
- grace is the first agent, which being freely participated by man, stirs and leads him or her out of every situation to the plenty of fruits of the truth but allowing its own order of doing;
- in the contemporary world the idea of effective grace as opposed to the thought of determination has the right to be proclaimed as a justifiable way proven by the huge number of examples - of which Augustine is an authoritative representative - and fully open to be experienced by all people of good will.

References

Abramowiczówna, Z. (ed.) 1965. *Słownik Grecko-Polski.* Warszawa: Państwowe Wydawnictwo Naukowe.

Augustine. *Confessions and Enchiridion*: 2015. At: http://www.ccel.org/ccel/augustine/confessions.pdf; [accessed Decembre 21, 2015].

Catechism of the Catholic Church. 2015. At: http://www.scborromeo.org/ccc/p2s2c1a1.htm; second edition [accessed Decembre 21, 2015].

Cyril of Jerusalem. 2015. De Spiritu Sancto. In: Migne. 2015. *Patrologia Graeca*, 33, 931–935. 939-942. At: http://www.freerepublic.com/focus/f-religion/2886087/replies?c=1; [accessed Octobre 7, 2015].

Indiculus **[1].** 2015. In: H. Denzinger (et. al.) *Enchiridion symbolorum, definitionum et declarationum de rebus fidei et morum.* At: http://patristica.net/denzinger/#n100 [accessed Octobre 8, 2015; older numbering].

Indiculus **[2].** 2015. In: H. Denzinger (et. al.) *Enchiridion symbolorum, definitionum et declarationum de rebus fidei et morum.* At: http://patristica.net/denzinger/enchiridion-symbolorum.html; [accessed Octobre 8, 2015; newer numbering].

New American Bible. 2015. At: http://www.vatican.va/archive/ENG0839/__P134.HTM; [accessed Octobre10, 2015].

Reber, A. 2002. *Słownik Psychologii.* Warszawa: Wydawnictwo Naukowe Scholar.

Salij, J. 1986. Duchowość dominikańska. In: *Dominikanie. Szkice z dziejów zakonu.* Poznań: W drodze, pp. 11–34.

Taylor, Ch. 2012: Źródła podmiotowości. Narodziny tożsamości nowoczesnej. Warszawa: Wydawnictwo Naukowe PWN.

Tischner, J. 1999. *Drogi i bezdroża miłosierdzia*. Kraków: Wydawnictwo AA.

Wojtyła, K. 1987. Kazanie na 50-lecie śmierci Brata Alberta. In: *Liturgia Godzin. Codzienna modlitwa ludu Bożego*, vol. III. Poznań: Pallotinum (here translated by Godawa M.).

THE PROCESS OF FORGIVENESS: "NO MORE A SERVANT, BUT A SON"

Tomaž Erzar & Katarina Kompan Erzar, Ljubljana

The idea of forgiveness that consists in letting go of negative feelings and resentment against offenders has recently gained much attention and empirical support in various academic disciplines. It has been observed that forgiveness offered to perpetrators helps victims restore mental and physical well-being after harmful events (Toussaint and Webb 2005). It has also been inferred that if forgiveness can transform internal states such as resentment and anger, it can also transform relationships, families, communities, and even societies in conflict (Worthington 2005). However, not all researchers and theorists agree what is meant by forgiveness and how forgiveness should be practiced. The purpose of this article is to present tensions inherent in the idea of forgiveness and attempt to combine different view of forgiveness into a single picture.

1. Different views on forgiveness

Psychologists define forgiveness as an intrapsychic process or result of this process that helps free the victimized person from the traps of past negative experiences (McCullough et al. 2000). This so-called "therapeutic" forgiveness focuses on victims' successive steps of recovery and does not consider reconciliation with wrongdoers to be an integral part of the process (VanOyen et al. 2001). Lay people, on the other side, have always linked forgiveness with reconciliation between the parties, absolving the offender from consequences and forgetting the harm. This is also the view traditionally linked with the Christian idea of love toward one's enemies. According to the New Testament, Christians are to forgive their offending brothers as many as "seventy-seven times" (Matt 18:21-22). In fact, most people in the Western culture understand forgiveness as an unconditional command placed onto victims to forgive the offenders, regardless of their readiness to repent and offer compensation (Kearns and Fincham 2004).

Both views have their advantages and disadvantages. While the scholarly view lacks the familiarity and intuitiveness of the popular or traditional view, the latter easily becomes moralistic and inoperative, as the right of victims to seek justice is taken into account. Victims should have the right to seek justice and demand apology or compensation for the harm, before encouraged to forgive. However, if forgiveness is too closely linked with seeking justice, its moral potential is lost. The psychological forgiveness, on the other side, enables victims to move forward in their lives, abandon the position of victimhood and leave the "prison of hate". Its strength comes from leaving out the interpersonal aspect of forgiveness and focusing on the internal states of the one forgiving. In the popular view, the interpersonal aspect becomes prominent: victims and offenders should reconcile, and it is the duty of morally conscious people to enable reconciliation through forgiveness.

Recently, some theologians have sought to solve the tension within the traditional view of forgiveness by offering an alternative interpretation of the biblical doctrine of unconditional forgiveness. According to this new interpretation, to forgive another who has not repent is at best self-destructive, if not humanly impossible (Bash 2011). It is important not to harbor grudges and be willing to forgive, but it is wrong, they argue, to offer forgiveness to those who may continue to harm you and do not seek forgiveness. Argument in favor of conditional forgiveness often refers to examples of God's forgiveness that is said to be dependent on sinners' repentance. Why should Christians' forgiveness be any different?

2. The question of perspective: the Parable of the Prodigal Son

We have strong reasons to believe that forgiveness cannot be granted by those who still suffer injustices, fear their oppressors, are continually oppressed, or constantly fear for their lives. Among elderly survivors of the Holocaust, one can hardly find anyone who would embrace the idea of forgiveness. At best, they strive to forgive the younger generations for the atrocities committed by their parents' generations (Kahana et al. 2015).

This observation makes a strong point for the conditional view on forgiveness. One cannot but agree with Anthony Bash who writes that offering forgiveness unconditionally is "pastorally naïve and dangerous", because it imposes unnecessarily high burdens on victims and lets offenders get away with their wrongdoing (Bash 2011, 137). The defenders of the conditional view often point to the Biblical examples of forgiveness and argue that even God's forgiveness - which acts as a model for human forgiveness - is conditional upon the sinner's repentance. There is no bestowing of mercy upon those who persist in sin (John 20:23) or sin against the Holy Spirit (Matt 12:31).

Biblical sources, however, when considered in context, never offer an easy way out of the problem of justice and reconciliation between people (see for example the story of the woman caught in adultery in John 8: 1-11). In the famous Parable of the Prodigal Son the father who symbolically represents God the Father does not wait to see the signs of his son's repentance, but runs toward him filled with compassion, relief and love (Luke 15:11-32). One could hardly interpret the father's attitude as conditional, since the whole point is made to stress that the son was lost, but is now found. In the parable, regret and repentance are not pictured as God's conditions of forgiveness, but as human conditions for metanoia. Another detail in this parable shows us that conditioning of God's love is part of human existence, not part of God's forgiveness: when the older son returns from work in the fields and sees the scene of forgiveness, he protests in indignation because his sense of justice is hurt. Here again we see the human reaction in the name of obedience and servitude placing conditions on God's love and refusing to forgive the brother.

The moral of the parable thus points in three ways, depending on the perspective of the persons involved in the story: a) from the perspective of the prodigal son, one is offered forgiveness if one acknowledges one's faults, repents and thrusts himself into the Father's embrace; b) from the perspective of the heavenly Father, the ultimate goal is the return of the lost son, not the moralistic stance which states that all sins end up in ruin and repentance; c) from the perspective of the older son, forgiveness offered to younger brother not only seems undeserved, but is offensive to all who live with the master and obediently work for him. It is only this latter perspective which is conditional and also disturbingly moralistic.

The parable which portrays God's forgiveness as unconditional and human forgiveness as conditional thus ends with an unanswered problem. Readers of this Biblical text cannot help but identify with the older brother and are left to wonder how he could also be brought to forgive. The answer to this question hinges upon the change of perspective or position: if the older brother is to forgive the younger brother and enjoy his father's possessions, he must abandon the position of servant and become a true son, which also means that he must be able to see the return of his brother from the perspective of the Father (Rupnik 1996).

3. How to stop being a victim: the Parable of the Unforgiving Servant

Relying on the reading of the parable, we propose that the opposing views of forgiveness (conditional vs. unconditional and interpersonal vs. internal) be considered as representations of the inner tensions in the heart of everyone trying to forgive. They may also be seen as the consequence of the particular perspective we might best describe as "the servant's point of view". From the servant's perspective, the opposing aspects of forgiveness are incompatible. However, they join each other once we abandon the position of servant. They may thus be understood as phases of one long process during which one ceases to perceive oneself as servant/victim and assumes the position of one who is powerful, empathic and forgiving.

Here we refer to an interesting point made by Fred Keene who argues that the parables in the New Testament indicate that forgiveness is never expected from those who are in a lower societal position (Keene 1995). A debt is canceled to servants by a master, never in the New Testament are servants pictured as those who are in a position to cancel their master's debt. Keene also observes that Jesus on the cross while suffering the worst possible sort of humiliation and degradation doesn't offer forgiveness himself, but turns to his heavenly Father (Luke 23:34). This, for Keene, is the ultimate proof that one should not try to forgive while being victimized, which means that forgiveness is reserved for those who can afford it, because they are in the upper positions. In this way, Keene hopes to reconcile the conditional view of forgiveness with the unconditional one by placing the burden of unconditional forgiveness onto those who are in power and onto equals, while totally releasing from this command those in lower positions. Keene's solution makes sense because it reaffirms what psychologists have been pointing out: one cannot forgive and should not try to forgive if and when in a role of victim.

We now propose to use Keene's idea of two different societal positions to describe the change of perspective which takes place within one person, but with important interpersonal consequences. In the Parable of Unforgiving Servant (Matt 18:23-35), the huge debt of the servant is forgiven by the master; consequently, the servant is expected to cancel the small debt he holds against another servant. Since the servant refuses to cancel the debt owed to him by his fellow servant, he is rebuked by God. Both parts of this story speak clearly in favor of Keene's interpretation. When it comes to forgiveness between two persons in an unequal socioeconomic position, like master and his servant, only master forgives the servant, and not vice versa. On the contrary, when it comes to forgiveness among equals, one is commanded to forgive in like proportion to the amount forgiven and reconcile regardless of how the other person will react. The mistake committed by the servant in the parable consists in his forgetting the debt that has just been cancelled to him and in being merciless toward his fellow servant who is indebted to him.

If we now apply the interpretation from the Parable of the Prodigal Son onto this parable, we can see that the problem in both parables consists in the fact that the servant, despite the master's offer to become his equal, perseveres in the role of servant. The problem of the unforgiving servant consists less in his being selfish and greedy, but in his being voluntarily limited to the position of the one who is down, less capable and powerless and who as such cannot genuinely offer forgiveness to anyone.

This sinful attitude is very similar to the problem psychologists describe as victim mentality or self-imposed victimhood (de Vries 2014). Victim mentality is a state of mind of persons who live under constant inner pressure of being down and helpless. While at the time of real danger this position is justified and protective, because it offers protection from further pain, it can gradually become a permanent way of living. As a self-defined victim, one is not only entitled to compassion and always right, but also exempt from the command to forgive. As long as people see themselves as victims, their ability to forgive is not only very conditional, but in fact minimal. In the process of healing from injustice, however, victims are invited to move forward and assume the position of one who is capable of compassion toward offenders and who without second thought offers them forgiveness. Similarly, the servant is not only invited to open up to God's unconditional forgiveness, pardoned and embraced as equal, but is expected to give freely since he is no longer a servant, but God's partner or son.

4. How to become a son

What has been initially presented as opposing views (or different societal positions in Keene's interpretation), can now be described as a process during which a change of perspective or position is achieved within one's own psyche. This change is brought about by a gradual shift of focus from the focus on oneself to the focus on others. While it is wrong to urge victims to prematurely focus on others and neglect their own needs and pain, it is also wrong for victims to exclusively focus on themselves and gradually become self-imposed martyrs (Staub 2005).

Ideally, to abandon the lower position, the victim needs to realize that it is the offender who is in the lower position and in need of understanding, compassion and forgiveness. In this endeavor, two insights can be helpful for the victim (Enright 2001). First, the need to realize that in other relationships one was also offender and has inflicted pain to innocent people. There is no other better way to help us move beyond the role of victimhood than the remembrance of injustices we were the cause. Second, the need to be forgiven for these offenses. The memory of pain and injustice we caused other people to suffer serves to bring into our awareness the feelings of guilt and remorse we experienced or at least should experience as offenders. By getting in touch with the position of offender, we readily experience the need to be forgiven and can easily extend this newly awakened awareness onto our offenders. As we identify with our own offending deeds and remorseful feelings, we get the chance to identify with those who have offended us and be less reluctant to offer forgiveness. This is also how Christians ordinarily understand the Lord's Prayer. As we remember our being sinners and offenders, and our being forgiven, we identify with offenders of all kinds, beg for their pardon, and offer them pardon.

Researchers recently discovered an interesting feature of perceiving oneself as victim: not only is such a victim entitled to be helped and pitied, victimhood gives one an indiscriminate right to fight back (Zitek et al. 2010, 252). Put in another way, being a victim, sooner or later entails becoming an offender. In light of this danger, victims should be helped as soon as possible to recover from the position of helplessness and be able to open up again to the goodness around them. This move toward goodness, however, cannot be accomplished with premature moralistic injunctions to forgive which often burden and obscure the true Christian vision of forgiveness.

Exerting compassion toward offenders sometimes comes naturally. When hindered, it is most often because of anger, fear, prejudice, ideological hatred, or all of those. No one is more prone to experience these feelings than the victimized person. That is why one should not be forced to forgive while in the position of victim. Western culture places great emphasis on being kind to others, but not so much to ourselves. When asked directly, most people report that they are kinder to others than themselves (Neff 2003). The danger to offer forgiveness before its due time is thus very real. Very real is also the reaction of victimized persons against forgiveness, because in their minds forgiveness entails more suffering and more injustice. However, there is no bigger danger for victims than to become offenders, and prisoners of hate they initially set out to defeat. Victims cannot abandon their lower position and put their suffering behind unless they start to see themselves also as offenders who have been forgiven. By remembering being forgiven, victims, almost without conscious effort, abandon their position of entitlement and get in touch with goodness in them and around them. By the same token, the move from the lower position of helpless victimhood to sovereign freedom among equals is achieved. In Christian understanding one becomes the son, when one sees others as they are seen by the Father, that is, as sons and brothers, all equal and all in need of unconditioned forgiveness and compassion.

References

Bash, A. 2011. Forgiveness: A Re-appraisal. *Studies in Christian Ethics*, 24(2): 133–146.

Enright, R. D. 2001. *Forgiveness is a choice: A step-by-step process for resolving anger and restoring hope.* Washington, DC: American Psychological Association.

Kahana, E., Kahana, B. Goler, T. and Wolf, J. K. 2015. Forgiveness: Complexities and Paradoxes in the Context of Genocide and Slavery. In: Sheila C. Bibb (ed.), *Forgiveness or Revenge: Restitution or Retribution? Inter-Dis-*

ciplinary Press, e-format. ISBN 978-1-84888-358-1. Available at: http://www.interdisciplinary.net%2Fpublishing%2Fproduct%2Fforgiveness-or-revenge-restitution-or-retribution%2F&usg=AFQjCNG8KiPsaXF4G7SEeLX-cRtaq70IKxA (accessed October 15, 2015).

Kearns, J. N., and Fincham, F. D. 2004. A prototype analysis of forgiveness. *Personality and Social Psychology Bulletin*, 30: 838–855.

Keene, Frederick W. 1995. *S*tructures of Forgiveness in the New Testament. In: Carol J. Adams and Marie M. Fortune (eds.), *Violence against Women and Children: A Christian Theological Sourcebook*, New York: Continuum, pp. 121–134.

Kets de Vries, M. F. R. 2012. Are You a Victim of the Victim Syndrome? *Organizational Dynamics*, 43(2): 130–137. Available at: http://dx.doi.org/10.2139/ssrn.2116238 (accessed October 15, 2015).

McCullough, M. E., Pargament, K. I., and Thoresen, C. E. 2000. *Forgiveness: Theory, research and practice*. New York: Guilford Press.

Neff, K.D. 2003. Self-compassion: an alternative conceptualization of a healthy attitude toward oneself. *Self and Identity, 2*: 85–102.

Rupnik, M. 1996. *Gli si gettò al collo, Lectio divina sulla parabola del padre misericordioso.* Roma: Lipa.

Staub, E. 2005. Constructive Rather than Harmful Forgiveness, Reconciliation, and Ways to Promote Them after Genocide and Mass Killing. In: E.L. Worthington (ed.), *Handbook of Forgiveness*. New York: Routledge, pp. 443–459.

Toussaint, L., and Webb, J. R. 2005. Theoretical and empirical connections between forgiveness, mental health and well-being. In: E.L. Worthington (ed.), *Handbook of Forgiveness*, New York: Routledge, pp. 349–362.

VanOyen, C. W., Ludwig, T. E., & Vander Laan, K. L. 2001. Granting forgiveness or harboring grudges: Implications for emotion, physiology and health. *Psychological Science*, 12(2): 117–123.

Worthington, E. L. 2005. More questions about forgiveness: Research agenda for 2005-2015. In: E. L. Worthington (ed.), *Handbook of Forgiveness*, New York: Routledge, pp. 557–575.

Zitek, E. M., Jordan, A. H., Monin, B., and Leach, F. R. 2010. Victim Entitlement to Behave Selfishly. *Journal of Personality and Social Psychology*, 98(2): 245–255.

TRUTH AND COMPASSION WHEN REVERSING A LIFE DECISION

Roman Globokar, Ljubljana

1. Status quaestionis

Recently one of the more poignant issues within the Catholic Church is the inclusion of the divorced and remarried in the Church. From 4th to 25th of October 2015 the regular Synod of Bishops on the Family took place in Rome. About 370 participants (279 of whom had the right to vote) discussed the vocation and mission of the family in the Church and in the contemporary world. The extraordinary assembly of the Synod of Bishops in 2014 already brought up the question of including the divorced and remarried in the life of the Church communities. The fact is that a divorce and second civil marriage are becoming more common even among the practicing Catholics. This practice of course breaks the Church norm of the inseparability of a marital communion and therefore the divorced and remarried are not allowed to receive the sacraments. The expectations for the Synod's final document were very high. Many hoped that the Synod Fathers would find a solution for the reintegration of the divorced and remarried into Church communities (Kasper 2014; Jopp 2015; Lintner 2015). Others feared that the Church could have been swayed by the spirit of relativism and accept decisions devaluating the sanctity of marriage (Voderholzer 2014, Aymans 2015). In a sense, we can recognise a kind of tension between truth and compassion in this issue. We can see a divergence between the steadfast upholding of the ideal (the doctrine) and the approach of compassion with individuals.

Before the Synod, a conviction appeared in the general public that Pope Francis certainly wants to change Church practice in this field; furthermore, that he wants to facilitate the receiving of sacraments for numerous Catholics who have stumbled along the way in their life stories. He himself initiated certain steps in this direction: he declared the Jubilee Year of Mercy, he simplified the legal procedures in determining the annulment of marriage; he invited Cardinal Walter Kasper to hold a lecture for the cardinal assembly in February 2014; he stressed the necessity of pastoral solutions. Yet, he did not want to impose solutions through his authority, and instead he deliberately reinforced the meaning of the collegiality of bishops by giving decision-making authority to bishops worldwide (Speech on Collegiality, October 17, 2015).

As the regular Synod in October 2015 approached, the clearer it became that the majority of the Synod Fathers would not support radical changes affecting family life. It was clear that there would be no changes regarding the recognition and acceptance of homosexual relationships or the opposition to receiving of sacraments by the divorced and remarried was becoming more expressed. The prefect of the Congregation for the Doctrine of the Faith, Cardinal Gerhard Müller, sought to develop a profound theological argumentation against the so-called "pastoral" solutions. He stressed that pastoral solutions should be rooted in the dogmatics, in the teachings of the Church. The Church must stick to the teachings of Jesus as well as to its own tradition. "Doctrine and pastoral care are the same thing. Jesus Christ as pastor and Jesus Christ as teacher with his word are not two different people" (*La Stampa*, 25 February 2014).

Immediately before the Synod, a book with the suggestive title *Eleven Cardinals Speak on Marriage and Family: Essays from a Pastoral Viewpoint* was published (Aymans 2015). It presents the different standpoints explaining how the Church doctrine as well as its practice cannot change. At the beginning of the Synod, thirteen cardinals handed over to the Pope a letter expressing their disagreement with the methods of the running of the Synod and with the draft of the working document as it was outlined by the preparatory board.

The other party that seemed to be in the minority at the Synod, led by Cardinal Walter Kasper, tried to find pastoral solutions, allowing the divorced and remarried to receive the sacraments of Penitence and the Eucharist. In the process of finding these solutions, they were guided primarily by the principle of mercy. There should be an opportunity for a divorced and remarried person to receive the sacraments (Kasper 2014, 86–92).

Both views diverge at the question of whether the Church should, in the case of the divorced and remarried, emphasise Jesus' teaching (the truth) or his mercy. The German-speaking cardinals at the Synod under the leadership of Cardinal Schönborn from Vienna accepted the position that the doctrine, the mercy and the justice cannot contradict each other as they coexist in God. They were trying to elaborate a middle position and their proposal had a strong impact on the final document of the Synod.

In principle, it is true that there cannot be a contradiction between doctrine, mercy, and justice, but certain differences emerge when we try to find practical solutions depending on our emphasis on the letter of the doctrine or on the attitude of compassion.

In my opinion, the justification of the so-called "pastoral" solutions paid too little attention to the theological foundations. In this respect, Cardinal Müller certainly has a point. Pastoral solutions should never be limited to a pragmatic solution to difficult situations. They should be, along with all Church directions, embedded in the teachings of Jesus and in coherence with fundamental theological truth about human beings. While taking that into consideration, this might bring about ruptures with the current practice, which would not be for the first time in the history of Church. Let us think about cases regarding slavery, death penalty, religious freedom, equality of genders, etc.

2. A life decision as a unique and final determination

The topic of life decision was of particular interest to Klaus Demmer (1931–2014), one of the leading moral theologians after Vatican II. By making a life decision, an individual gives meaning to their life, thus decisively defining the rest of their life. It is the deepest, the innermost decision an individual can make for themselves. Demmer starts with an anthropological fact that a human being is somebody who searches for meaning, realising its own mortality and transience. They therefore wish to give their life path a final direction.

In the irrevocable life decision, a fundamental decision (*optio fundamentalis*) is paradigmatically incarnated as an inclination of an acting person towards the good on a transcendental level. It is the innermost concretisation of the fundamental decision in the life of every individual. All following decisions are conditioned with this decision. It is a unique and irrevocable decision that cannot be seen merely as "a single act but rather a lifelong process of realising oneself in a creative way and in an ever growing liberated determination" (Demmer 1974, 257–258). In spite of that, this self-determination focuses in a single moment in one's life. Considering past experience and conscientious reflection, they determine their future.

What is the foundation for the singularity of a life decision? According to Demmer, it is the fact that life itself is unique and unrepeatable, aimed to its end, and therefore an individual wishes to give it a final meaning, even with a step into the unknown. The man feels small and limited and it is his awareness of limitations and transience that inspires him to give his life a lasting mark. In the moment of a life decision, individuals do not choose something outside of themselves; they decide about themselves. They choose themselves in their own unique personal history: "The life decision requires that a person's entire life be totally identified with the conditions of her or his particular vocation; it so uniquely stands for the singularity of a person's life that she or he comes to recognize her or his very self *in* her or his life decision" (Demmer 2000, 52).

We are talking about the ability to determine oneself: "Out of the multitude of possible realisations he chooses the one he is convinced best suits him while at the same time forsaking all others" (Demmer 1974, 21). Demmer is convinced that human fate is not predetermined and that humans are free and determine significantly the course of their life paths. While doing so they are not in possession of a complete and clear understanding, and therefore in any case take on a certain amount of risk, as they are finite, temporal creatures, limited and fallible in their understanding and judgement. Therefore, a life decision always carries only the character of a moral certitude that "under no circumstance excludes the possibility of a mistake and an alternative solution" (Demmer 1974, 37). We do not have objective certainty but rather personal certainty of our life's realisation.

In spite of that, Demmer is convinced that every human being must come to a life decision moment in its life. "At some point all the necessary conditions giving way to a final determination of one's life must be fulfilled" (Demmer 1974, 25). Without the conscientious decision, one could not live their life to the fullest and would be left wandering and aimless. "A step into the unknown, into the incomprehensible is actively a waypoint in the biography of every spiritually aware human being" (Demmer 2014, 50). As a given personal existence is unique and unrepeatable, "so can man only once and unrepeatably unite with his existence while taking a single life decision as a gift. One commits to himself only once!" (1974, 183). This raises the question of how would Demmer judge a second marriage in the case of the death of the first spouse or induction into a monastery following the death of a spouse. Would be this considered a rupture with the life decision?

Within the Catholic Church, we know three institutionalised forms of life decision that "enjoy public canonical protection: marriage, priesthood, and religious life". "Besides these three classical states, private forms of consecration may call for an irrevocable life choice, at least in specific cases: for example, a person may discover her or his vocation in a particular profession and bind her or his entire life to it" (Demmer 2000, 52). With the institutionalised forms of life decision the private decision gains public value and protection, while non-institutionalised decisions remain privately intimate. Nevertheless, we may speak of the possibility of infidelity to a life decision even in this regard.

The personal truth is never concluded for good but requires constant reaffirmation and maturation. "Once the choice is made, what follows is essentially the constant struggle to confirm the choice, to mature in it, to spiritually articulate its potential for happiness and fulfilment, and to translate it into daily life" (Demmer 2000, 52).

Even moments of crisis provide opportunity for someone to deepen and purify his life decision. In the first period Demmer highly stressed the tutioristic principle, meaning it is necessary to insist on a chosen life decision. Only in extreme circumstances when there is absolutely no alternative is an external relinquishment of a chosen life decision allowed. This is true especially in cases where the initial decision was wrong or mistaken. "The moral capacity of a man is not limitless, it is impossible to permanently live with a wrong decision if you do not want to impoverish yourself and demise" (Demmer 1974, 144).

In the last stages of his life Demmer also suggested as a solution the possibility of a dispensation for married couples, similarly as it is arranged for priests and members of religious orders and congregations. "It is scandalous that the marriage, the promise of celibacy, and religious vows are treated differently. The will for a bounding commitment is the same in all the cases" (2014, 82). From the standpoint of moral theology, there is no difference between a sacramental and a non-sacramental life decision. The level of irrevocability is the same.

The dispensation is an act of mercy towards an individual. It has its boundaries because it cannot lose sight of the common good of the Church. To prevent scandals in the Church, the dispensation must be limited, or rather its boundaries clearly set. While bestowing dispensation the Church can lean on the Gospel, specifically on the Sermon on the Mount. The basic guideline should be: "When in doubt, favour the mercy" (Demmer 2014, 82). We must clearly point out that Demmer never in any sense advocated for a lax approach. An individual is never entitled to remarry. But if they reached through spiritual counselling after a period of penitence the conclusion that they feel they could receive the Eucharist, the Church should allow that. At the same time, Demmer adds that the first responsibility of the Church community is in profound preparation for the sacrament of marriage that should be led by experienced married couples. The competent moral theologian also encourages their colleagues and Church teachings to learn from the small steps, a pedagogy that shields us from almost unachievable and too high expectations. "The high expectations set by the Gospel must not wither. The existence of faith and Church in the pluralistic and predominantly relativistic general public is based on this condition. The required attitude does not however exclude an empathic compassion for individual cases. ... One must be able to carry on, on his life path, both theoretically and practically" (Demmer 2014, 193).

3. Opening a new perspective

The current understanding and Church teachings on the indissolubility of marriage is neither a dogma nor a final teaching. The moderation of the Church practice needs a solid theological foundation. Only the so-called pastoral solutions cannot face in an appropriate manner the complexity of the challenge. A renewed theology of family and marriage from a personalistic point of view is required. Following the tradition, an Apostolic Exhortation on the conclusions of the Synod on Family 2015 is expected by Pope Francis. The Final Report of the Synod in Article 85 leaves the door slightly ajar to the continued reflection on the position of the divorced and remarried in the Church. "Therefore, while supporting a general rule, it is necessary to recognize that responsibility with respect to certain actions or decisions is not the same in all cases. Pastoral discernment, while taking into account properly formed conscience of a person, must take responsibility for these situations. Even the consequences of actions taken are not necessarily the same in all cases." (Synod of Bishops 2015, Art. 85) This article was barely confirmed by a two-third majority with 178 Synod Fathers voting for and 80 against it.

In my opinion, *discernment* can be identified as the keyword of the Synod. The request for discernment is expressed in different articles of the Final Report regarding different areas. Let us just list Articles dealing with discernment: 3, 29, 35, 47, 51–53, 57–58, 69, 75, 84–86. In Articles 51 and 85, there is a direct quotation from *Familiaris Consortio,* 84, written by Pope John Paul II: "Pastors must know that, for the sake of truth, they are obliged to exercise careful discernment of situations." However, John Paul II in his Apostolic Exhortation from 1981 came in the same Article 84 to the conclusion that, "The Church reaffirms her practice, which is based upon Sacred Scripture, of not admitting to Eucharistic Communion divorced persons who have remarried." Not including this part of *Familiaris Consortion* in the Final Report of the Synod in 2015 can be interpreted as an indication that careful discernment can also lead to a different conclusion. It is not directly written that the Church practice regarding the divorced and remarried should change, but there are enough elements in the Final Report to pave the way for the sacramental inclusion of these people in the life of the Church. The attitude of Pope Francis gives positive signs in this direction. In his closing address to the Synod Fathers, he strongly emphasised the principle of mercy. He used the word truth only once, whereas the word mercy nine times. (In the Final Report of the Synod, the word truth is used 22 times, the word mercy 25 times.) The following statement is also very suggestive: "The Synod experience also made us better realise that the true defenders of doctrine are not those who uphold its letter, but its spirit; not ideas but people; not formulae but the gratuitousness of God's love and forgiveness" (Francis 2015).

References

Aymans, W. (ed.) 2015. *Eleven Cardinals Speak on Marriage and Family: Essays from a Pastoral Viewpoint.* San Francisco: Ignatius.

Demmer, K. 1974. *Die Lebensentscheidung: ihre Moraltheologischen Grundlagen.* Paderborn: Schöningh.

Demmer, K. 2000. *Shaping the Moral Life: An Approach to Moral Theology.* Washington: Georgetown University Press.

Demmer, K. 2014. *Selbstaufklärung theologischer Ethik: Themen – Thesen – Perspektiven*. Paderborn: Ferdinand Schöningh.

Francis. 2015. Conclusion of the Synod of Bishops: Address of his Holiness Pope Francis. Vatican City (October 24). In: http://w2.vatican.va/content/francesco/en/speeches/2015/october/documents/papa-francesco_20151024_sinodo-conclusione-lavori.html (January 18, 2016).

Globokar, R. 2015. Lebensentscheidung als endgültige Bestimmung der eigenen Zukunft: zur Stellung der Lebensentscheidung in der Moraltheologie Klaus Demmers. *Bogoslovni vestnik*, 75(3): 447—460.

John Paul II. 1981. *Apostolic Exhortation Familiaris Consortio*. In: http://w2.vatican.va/content/john-paul-ii/en/apost_exhortations/documents/hf_jp-ii_exh_19811122_familiaris-consortio.html (January 18, 2016)

Jopp, A. 2015. *Es ist Zeit: Kommunion für wiederverheiratete Geschiedene jetzt!* Oberursel: Publik-Forum.

Kasper, W. 2014. *Das Evangelium von der Familie: die Rede vor dem Konsistorium*. Freiburg: Herder.

Lintner, M. 2015. Vprašanje razvezanih in ponovno poročenih od koncila do danes. *Bogoslovni vestnik* 75 (3): 461–474.

Synod of Bishops. 2015. The Final Report of the Synod of Bishops to the Holy Father, Pope Francis. Vatican City (October 24). In: http://www.vatican.va/roman_curia/synod/documents/rc_synod_doc_20151026_relazione-finale-xiv-assemblea_en.html (January 18, 2016).

Voderholzer, R. (ed.) 2014. *Zur Seelsorge wiederverheirateter Geschiedener: Dokumente, Kommentare und Studien der Glaubenskongregation.* Würzburg: Echter.

MISUSE OF TRUTH IN THE MARRIAGE AND ITS FATAL CONSEQUENCES

Stanislav Slatinek, Ljubljana

1. Introduction

Sincerity of spouses is of great importance for a Christian marriage, which extends to all areas of husband and wife's life, including the most intimate. Therefore, the specific duty of spouses is that they tend from the very outset of the marriage to be concluded in mutual sincerity and in love of truth. Only then spouses can "mutually give and accept one another for the purpose of establishing a marriage" in an irrevocable covenant (Can. 1057 §2). Matrimonial community, which has been put together in the love of truth, is characterized by personal satisfaction, which is full of creativity. Nevertheless, we canot avoid the danger that in a marriage "the truth is being abused" (Slatinek 2015/a, 265–274). Roman jurist Ulpian already warned against the danger if the marriage is concluded on the basis of deceitful fraud.[1] Matrimonial relationships should be free. The decision to marry should be the result of free will, on the basis of which fiancées express their agreement. Each fraud causes a void marriage. Therefore, we are talking about void marriages on the account of deceitful fraud.

2. The dimensions of the deceitful fraud

Deceitful fraud (*deceptus dolo*) in the marriage means that the personal qualities are knowingly and willingly described in such a way that the audience is being intrigued. Qualities that are important for the marriage are being described. The fraud lies in the fact that the described properties (if they really existed or if they did not exist at all) would be very disruptive to the marriage and the spouse would decide completely different if he/she knew the whole truth. Properties that can be very disturbing for the Christian marriage are for example: suicide attempt (Slatinek 2015/b, 143–150), drug abuse, homosexual disposition, mental illness, alcoholism, infertility, impotence, false or concealed pregnancy, infec-

1 D. 4.3.1.2. http://droitromain.upmf-grenoble.fr/Corpus/d-04.htm#3 (obtained Decembre 13, 2015).

tion with HIV, belonging to non-Christian sect, pre-fatherhood or motherhood and the like (Coram Defilippi 1997, 856). Those who deceit, are not necessarily only the future spouses. It may also be a third party (such as a parent, a relative or a friend), who upsets with his lying talk so much, that the other party agrees to marriage. Acts that are committed on the account of deception fraud are valid themselves in canon law. At the request of a damaged party or by official duty, those acts can be repealed by the judgment of the judge (Can. 125 §2).

Deceitful fraud must be distinguished from error (*error*). A simple error hinders freedom of action, to obstruct valid (matrimonial) contract. A person that is wrong behaves differently than he/she would act if he/she knew the whole truth. For deceitful fraud, it is a much more serious thing. The fraud does not only affect the will and intellect, but also hurts dignity. With deceit, one side is trying for the other side to reach the conclusion of the (marriage) contract with illegal means. Therefore, the fraud is a wicked, malicious and offensive plan, by which the other person wants to be deceived and tricked in order to achieve a certain action. Because of the fraud, a good deed also becomes bad, shameful and void in itself, as the Roman proverb says: "A contract cannot be generated from the crime" (*ex maleficio non oritur contractus*).[2]

Although a fraud differs from the error, they are usually acting together. By that, two criteria are important: evaluation criteria (*criterium aestimationis*) and response criteria (*criterium reactionis*). When a matrimonial contract is to be made by fraud, a fiancé "estimates" if his/her partner has or has not a desired personal property. And if he/she finds that a desired personal property is absent, they "react" with sadness, anger, crying and asking for the marriage to be dissolved immediately.

Purpose of the deception in marriage is to achieve consent (*consensus*). All other purposes (for example, to obtain a pecuniary advantage, good name, social influence, nationality, etc.) have no weight and do not cause defects in consent to the matrimony. Although the marriage of a man and a woman is something good, it is something bad in the case of a fraud, because the fraudster intention is to trick someone into the marriage. Normally, the person who is being seduced with the trick would never marry if he/she had all the knowledge. Therefore, the matrimonial consent obtained by deception is void (Stankiewicz 2003, 179; Maria Punzi Nicolò 2003, 195), because out of a fraud no marriage can occur.

2 D. 46.1.70.5. http://droitromain.upmf-grenoble.fr/Corpus/d-46.htm#1 (obtained Decembre 13, 2015).

Deceitful fraud is also unfair because it persuades a fiancé into marriage in a shameful and insulting manner. Due to that fraud, the tricked fiancé decides for a marriage that will never become a loving one. It is only a mere coexistence of two persons, who cause each other a lot of physical and mental suffering. Such marriage disintegrates because the truth is different from the one described by the fraudster (Coram Faltin 1998, 437).

When all of these criteria overlap, a deceitful fraud occurs, which nullifies the matrimony (Can. 1098). Presumptions are not sufficient to prove such scams. In proving deceitful frauds, all available and legitimate means and methods are to be used, such as a judicial hearing of the parties, the submission of medical and other documents, as well as the interrogation of witnesses who know the case already before the procedure and can testify the facts relied on by the plaintiff (Bianchi 1996, 376). Persons who have caused the deception and their witnesses do not normally respond to the invitation of the Court and are uncooperative in the litigation of matrimonial annulment. A major problem in proving a deceitful fraud is also the medical documentation, which is confidential. Hospitals and treatment centers are issuing documents only in specific cases and at the request of the treated persons. If the person who caused the deception was treated for a disease that was concealed to the spouse, its proving largely depends on the medical records. Therefore, all the more should annulling legal proceedings be conducted with full responsibility and in accordance with legal regulations. Only so damage and injustice caused by misuse of the truth can in some cases be repaired.

3. Example of case law: concealed infertility

How fatal the deceitful fraud for a marriage can be, we read in the judgments of the court of Roman Rota and provincial courts. Since 1983, the Roman Rota often dealt with the deceitful fraud in the litigations of matrimonial annulments (Mingardi, 2008, 185). Between 1995 and 2005, the Roman Rota assessed in 22 cases if the marriage is void on the account of deception fraud. The high number of deception frauds is recorded in the provincial ecclesiastical courts. In the discussion, we would like to present a case Coram Silvestri (Silvestri 2004, 19-44), of the Provincial Court of Campana, which describes concealed infertility.

Anton got sick in his childhood. When he was ten years old, his doctors diagnosed criptorchidism (from Greek κρυπτός, kryptos which means *to hide* and ὄρχις, orchis, testis). The treating physician told Anton's mother that Anton needed to be treated; otherwise he will remain infertile at a young age due to improper developed testes. Anton has been treated for some time, but later abandoned the treatment because his parents were separating. Children's doctor constantly reminded that Anton is going to be having problems in adulthood if treatment is not continued. Due to problems in his family, Anton spent his youth without medical care. As he turned twenty, he met Dora and they got engaged. Dora has repeatedly expressed her desire that she wants to have many children in matrimony. After one year of acquaintance, they got married. Since several years after the marriage they had no children, Dora started the treatments and encouraged Anthony to visit the doctors. Anton resisted this for a long time, finally, he admitted to Dora that due to neglected childhood disease he remained sterile.

Anton knew all the time that Dora wanted to have children. Before and after the wedding he did not have the courage to tell Dora the truth about his condition. His silence was not accidental. He remained silent, knowingly and intentionally in order to conceal his infertility. His silence knowingly misled Dora into error and it concealed the fact that he is sterile. Only after one year of Dora's treatment, he admitted that because of the diagnosis criptorchidism he remained infertile.

Dora had a lot of brothers and sisters. Therefore, she herself wanted to have many children. When she married Anton, she has repeatedly expressed the desire that she wants children. She was convinced that Anton is fertile and that they could have a big family. When they talked about children, Anton silently listened. Occasionally, however, he suggested that first they should arrange the house and that afterwards they would have children.

Anton's admission that he was infertile shocked Dora and she immediately demanded the separation of marriage. She felt affected, cheated and misconducted. The lack of children was unacceptable for Dora because she did not want a marriage without children and she would never be with Anton if she knew for his infertility.

Dora filed a case at the provincial court in Campana (Italy) in order to litigate invalidity of the marriage because of Anton's concealed infertility. The judges placed a disputed question whether this case is a fraud (*dolus malus*), whereas the defendant intentionally committed an evil act by hiding his infertility, and deceived Dora into the marriage. If the plaintiff would know of his infertility from the beginning, she would never marry him because she always wanted to have many children in her matrimony.

4. Legal position on concealed infertility

Fraud (*dolus malus*) is a very common form of deception fraud in marriage. The court practice of the court of Roman Rota recorded a large percentage of deceitful frauds - while entering a marriage certain features that can interfere a matrimonial community are concealed. Example Coram Silvestri describes concealed infertility, which is a severe interference in the very essence of a marriage. One of the essential purposes of the Christian marriage is in fact the birth (*prolis generationem*) and the education of children (Can. 1055). When one spouse knows that this goal cannot be achieved, and conceals that truth knowingly, he commits an act of omission (*actum omissum*) to achieve egoistic goal of obtaining marital consent. Therefore, the case Coram Silvestri is an act of shameful, harmful and evil deceitful fraud. The Court in that case held that it was not only a fraud (*dolus malus*), but also knowingly misleading in another deceitful error (*error dolosus*).

In the case of Coram Silvestri, it has been proven that the defendant excluded the honesty in marriage. For a happy marriage, the honesty of spouses is essential. If one of the spouses at the time of engagement conceals their properties, they knowingly cause an error on the personal characteristics by the second spouse. Deceitful hiding of one's personal qualities, as seen in the case of Coram Silvestri, means that with the evasions, deafness, numbness and suppressing the truth, one creates a false belief that everything is in order. Therefore, any subsequent recognition seriously affects a community of spouses (*consortium vitae*). Canon Law therefore strongly defends the rights of spouses to be properly trained and that before the conclusion of marriage they would not be concealed anything, which would later by its very nature utterly disrupt their matrimonial happiness.

From the judgments of the court of Roman Rota, it is obvious that when entering the marriage, various physical and mental diseases are being deceived. In the case of Coram Silvestri, the defendant knowingly concealed his infertility (*sterilitas matrimonium*), which is one of the worst forms of deceitful scams and may significantly disturb the matrimonial union. Although infertility of one of the spouses is no obstacle to the conclusion of the Christian marriage, it can cause many problems for a happy marriage, especially when one of the spouses consciously wants to have many children.

Birth ability i.e. fertility (*fertilitas*) is a very important feature for a marriage. Even in the case of Coram Silvestri, the plaintiff wanted the defendant to be fertile, so that they would be able to have children. Therefore, on this basis deceitful frauds should not happen. When one person is barren, and the other is extremely keen to have children and infertility is deliberately withhold, an error on the characteristics of a person as well as the deceitful fraud occurs. Matrimonial fertility in the case of Coram Silvestri was not only naturally demanded, but its absence severely undermined the confidence in the sincerity of the defendant, which made the marriage to be disintegrated and annulled by the Regional Court in Campana.

5. How to prevent deceitful fraud - practical principles

The civil society and the Church in particular are required to ensure measures in order to minimize fraudulent and unfair marriages. Here are some practical principles:

- Many dioceses around the world seek even more appropriate forms of preparation for marriage. Longer preparation is very important; it comprises the childhood and it is primarily happening in the domestic family. The education of the children begins before birth and continues throughout growing age. Parents are the primary educators of their children, when educating for the Christian virtues, among which honesty and truthfulness are very important. Such children are taught at a young age to speak the truth. A child who is cheating, scheming and is treacherous, will behave fraudulent and deceitful (*dolosus*) later also as a fiancé. It is therefore important that children at an early age of their growing up learn to describe their characteristics honestly, without any exaggeration and embellishment.
- Among educational issues, sex education of children received from their parents in the age of adolescence is very important. Today we are concerned to note that many parents provide a permissive upbringing of their children, where issues of sexuality are not included in the educational process. Even greater problems are in the families where children are victims of sexual violence. It is therefore necessary to strengthen the youth ministry, which will create suitable environment for a relaxing and informative conversation about human sexuality.
- The complete process of education, which includes all issues that are important to the marriage, must be at the heart of the catechists, animators and especially priests – parish priests in particular. It is necessary to look for ever new forms of evangelization, that the young people who are called into marriage deeply understand issues related to sexuality, love and sexual abstinence, and that they will have enough opportunity to speak even about their own trauma (sexual violence of minors by parents or relatives) and the family secrets (sexual or hereditary diseases present in the family).
- Especially in the period of the nearing preparation for the marriage (time of engagement), young people need help to overcome selfishness and to learn a sincere conversation and complete donation. This is a precious time when one needs to help young people to discover the great value of the sacrament of Reconciliation and the Eucharist. For the preparation of fiancées, it is good to include as many professionally qualified people, preferably experts in medicine, law, psychology and priests.

- Priority attention should be paid to the immediate preparation of the fiancées (Slatinek 2014, 16–18). Direct preparation for a marriage must contain questions to ensure that the fiancées know each other enough and that they are really willing to marry freely. Emeritus Pope Benedict XVI often thought about that. On the preparation of fiancées, he says: "Among the means for ascertaining whether the project of the Engaged couple is truly conjugal the prematrimonial examination stands out. This examination has mainly a juridical purpose: to ascertain that nothing impedes the valid and licit celebration of the wedding. However, juridical does not mean formal, as though it were a bureaucratic step, like filling up a form based on a set questions. Instead it is a unique pastoral opportunity - one to be made the most of with the full seriousness and attention that it requires - and which, through a dialogue full of respect and cordiality, the pastor seeks to help the person to face seriously the truth about himself or herself and about his or her own human and Christian vocation for marriage. In this sense the dialogue, always conducted separately with each of the engaged pair without lessening the possibility of further conversations with the couple - requires an atmosphere of full sincerity and which stress should be put on the fact that the contracting parties themselves are those first concerned and first obliged in conscience to celebrate a valid marriage." (Acta Benedicti Pp. XVI. 2011, 111) Only in this way, with various means that are available for careful preparation for the marriage, one can develop effective matrimonial ministry, which can interrupt, as far as possible, the vicious circle of deceitful fraud and a growing number of void marriages.
- Direct preparation for marriage must necessarily include also the interpretation of some very important issues, such as unity, indissolubility and the importance of faith in the marriage. "The indissoluble pact between a man and a woman does not, for the purposes of the sacrament, require of those engaged to be married, their personal faith; what it does require, as a necessary minimal condition, is the intention to do what the Church does "(Acta Benedicti Pp. XVI. 2013, 169). As the International Theological Commission observed and a Document of 1977: "Where there is no trace of faith (in the sense of the term 'belief' - being disposed to believe), and no desire for grace or salvation is found, then a real doubt arises as to whether there is the above-mentioned and truly sacramental intention and whether in fact the contracted marriage is validly contracted or not." (2.3) The engaged person should be warned about the dangers, which arise if any of the fiancées who is without faith, abuses the truth and has deceitful purpose to conceal the truth about him/herself in order to reach the matrimonial consent. A fiancé, who wants to deceive in order to achieve the matrimonial

consent, is unfair to the other fiancé and to the children. Children who are born in marriage deserve honest parents who are truthful and honest with one another. Due to the deceitful scams, children usually suffer the most.

- For successful marriages, in which there are no tricks, nor cheating, a permanent tendance of the married couples is also useful. Marital groups and regular therapy sessions can help spouses to maintain and cultivate matrimonial love, mutual matrimonial communication and virtues of married life. Thus, even in the marriage some painful sores from a young age (dishonesty, lies and fraud) can be treated.

Abbreviations

Coram – in front of the named judge of the Roman Rota.
D. – *Digesta seu Pandectae.* A name for a legal compendium, which consists the *Corpus Iuris Civilis Romani.*
RRDec. – *Rotae Romanae Tribunal. Decisiones seu sententiae.* Città del Vaticano: Libreria Editrice Vaticana.
ZCP – *Code of Canon Law.* 1983. Ljubljana: Human Rights Press.

References

Acta Benedicti Pp. XVI. 2011. Ad sodales Tribunalis Rotae Romanae. In: *AAS* 103/2:108–113.
– – –. 2013. Ad Romanae Rotae Tribunal. In: *AAS* 105/2:168–172.
Bianchi, P. 1996. Esempi di applicatione giurisprudenziale del can. 1098 (dolo): casistica e problemi probatori. In: *Quaderni di Diritto Ecclesiale* 9:357–378.
Coram Defilippi, judgment on 4th of December 1997. In: *RRDec.*, 89:853–865.
Coram Faltin, judgment on 3rd of June 1998. In: *RRDec.,* 90:434–443.
Corpus Iuris Civilis. 1829. *Iustiniani Digesta*: *Gaius libro primo de verborum obligationibus,* vol. I. *46.1.70.5.* http://droitromain.upmf-grenoble.fr/Corpus/d-46.htm#1 (accessed December 13, 2015).
Corpus Iuris Civilis. 1829. *Iustiniani Digesta*: *Ulpianus libro 11 ad edictum,* vol. I. *4.3.1.2.* http://droitromain.upmf-grenoble.fr/Corpus/d-4.htm#1 (accessed December 13, 2015).
International Theological Commission. 1977. *Propositions on the Doctrine of Christian Marriage.* http://www.vatican.va/roman_curia/congregations/cfaith/cti_documents/rc_cti_1977_sacramento-matrimonio_en.html (accessed December 13, 2015).
Maria Punzi Nicolò, A. 2003. La qualitas quae natura sua consortium vitae coniugalis perturbare potest (can. 1098). In: P. Antonio Bonnet & C. Gullo

(eds.), *Diritto matrimoniale canonico*: *Il consenso*, vol. II, Libreria Editrice Vaticana: Città del Vaticano, pp. 191–199.

Mingardi, M. 2008. L'errore di fatto, spontaneo e doloso (cann. 1097 e 1098). In: *Quaderni di Diritto Ecclesiale* 11/2:184–205.

Silvestri, P. 2004. *La nullità del matrimonio canonico. Raccolta di sentenze.* Napoli: Guida.

Slatinek, S. 2014. *Izgubljeni prstan: Kako pomagati ločenim in znova poročenim kristjanom.* Maribor: Ognjišče, Slomškova založba.

– – –. 2015/a. Zloraba resnice v zakonski zvezi. *Bogoslovni vestnik* 75:265–274.

– – –. 2015/b. Suicidal Ideation in Relationships prior to Marriage and Its Impact on Decisions Whether a Marriage between Such Couples can be Annulled. In: J. Juhant, B. Žalec (eds.), *Understanding Genocide and Suicide*. Zürich & Berlin: Lit 2015, pp. 143–151.

Stankiewicz, A. 2003. La fattispecie di errore doloso prevista dal can. 1098. In: P. Antonio Bonnet & C. Gullo (eds.), *Diritto matrimoniale canonico*: *Il consenso*, vol. II, Libreria Editrice Vaticana: Città del Vaticano, pp. 177–190.

ABSTRACTS

Robert Petkovšek
RENUNCIATION OF LIE – WAY OUT OF VIOLENCE

Abstract: René Girard attributes the origin of man to mimetic desire, which is contrary within itself, at once a creative and destructive force. The history of humanity is thus not only a history of progress but also a history of violence. The role of the institution of ritual sacrifice and scapegoat, which Girard recognizes as the original and fundamental institution, has been to control, restrain and avert violence from its tendency to extremes. As human institutions have been weakening in the last centuries evil has begun to manifest itself in its extreme and demonic forms and threatens modern globalized society through the possibility of apocalyptic self-destruction of humanity. This article discusses the relationship between violence and truth, which is the principal opponent of violence, according to Pascal. Violence and truth, which meet throughout human existence, have a paradoxical relationship. Special attention is given to the point at which violence exceeds anthropological bounds and becomes demonic. Demonic violence turns man into an un-human. Authors such as Aleksandr Solzhenitsyn and Alain Besançon help elucidate the role of lies in the escalation of demonic violence. Nazi and communist totalitarianism institutionalized lie in the form of ideology and political system in order to legitimize and protect violence. Institutionalized lie is the consequence of human inaction and indifference to truth. Active renunciation of lie makes it possible to leave this circle of violence.

Key words: violence, demonic, apocalyptic, lie, truth, René Girard, Blaise Pascal, Aleksandr Solzhenitsyn, Alain Besançon, Carl von Clausewitz.

Bojan Žalec
HUMAN REFUSAL OF THE BASIC TRUTH ABOUT SELF AS THE ORIGIN OF VIOLENCE

Abstract: Charles K. Bellinger is a contemporary American theologian. A lucid and penetrative thinker and connoisseur, he is original at interpreting and advancing the findings of Søren Kierkegaard, Eric Voegelin and René Girard. This essay presents Bellinger's account of dangerous, harmful and violent pathological states and actions that originate in disturbances in three inseparably linked dimensions of human life: first, the vertical dimension, which consists of the relationship between the human and God; second, the temporal trajectory of development or non-development of the human self (the "I"); third, the horizontal or societal dimension. Bellinger founds his claims upon special theological anthropology, which in turn is grounded on Kierkegaard's findings that Bellinger interprets and applies to modern and contemporary phenomena. This forms a basis for the author to establish a link between the human refusal to accept the basic truth about self and the violent and non-compassionate character of his actions.

Key words: Bellinger, Kierkegaard, theological anthropology, three dimensions of reality and human life, refusal of God's call to spiritual growth or becoming an image of God, single individual, crowd is untruth, forms of insanity, violence and non-compassion.

Stanko Gerjolj
"HE DESCENDED INTO HELL": PEDAGOGICAL AND PSYCHOLOGICAL DIMENSION OF TRUTH AND COMPASSION

Abstract: In the Apostolic Creed, before his resurrection, Jesus takes us "before Hell". This path is often set off by educators, counsellors and psychotherapists, when they emphatically entirely approach the "Hell of untruth and lies", in which there are people who are seeking for help. Based on "Hell", Communism wanted to create "Heaven", which like the Tower of Babel began to tear down with the fall of the Berlin Wall. In these burnt areas there are still many parts where wars are raging and tensions prevailing. Even in the Slovenian region there are still strong waves of smoke billowing from the burnt area. A key dimension in the quest for truth is compassionate empathy with both the perpetrators of "Hell" as well as with those who were pushed into it. In "Hell", the truth is in fact misrepresented while people are silent or not allowed to speak about the real truth. Compassionate empathy enables a breakthrough to experiential truth, which in itself opens the way towards the actual truth. In the hellish period of Communism there were many hidden truths, even between parents and children. Selective silence harms honest communication more than a direct lie. We have learned to carry this "silence of the truth" from one generation to another. Significant changes have led us in a context where the path to – experiential and objective – truth is increasingly opening up. But along the way, we will certainly meet "before Hell". We can only hope that we travel with enough compassion and empathy to find a way of hope in a different, more "redeemed" and liberated future.

Key words: Communism, suppressed truth, silence, compassion, experiential truth.

Marcel V. Măcelaru

TRUTH, JUSTICE, UPRIGHTNESS: HUMAN FLOURISHING IN PROPHETIC PERSPECTIVE

Abstract: The concept of Human Flourishing has been much debated and opinions on what it entails vary. This study takes a theological stance on the matter – it is argued that besides physical and emotional concerns, true flourishing necessitates spiritual wellbeing. As such, it can only be attained by participation in a biblically defined covenantal nexus of relationships, whereby relating rightly to God, neighbour and creation is the divinely intended mode of existence. Jeremiah's prophetic call to truth, justice and uprightness (Jer. 4:2) is but one example where such existence is sponsored.

Key words: human flourishing, theological existence, life with God, personhood, truth, justice, uprightness, prophecy of Jeremiah.

Anton Jamnik

TRUTH AND COMPASSION – HUMAN DIGNITY, THE ETHICAL NORM WHICH SHOULD BE RESPECTED BY ALL PERSONS

Abstract: We live in a plural democratic society. Democracy is not only a political form of co-existence; this is, in fact, a way of thinking, advocated by the individuals and society. Democratic thought emphasises individual freedom. The entire society strives to provide as much freedom as possible to each of its citizens. One of the necessary pre-conditions for a peaceful co-existence within a plural democratic society is tolerance, i.e. respect for various opinions. Within democracy there exist various interpretations as regards morally-admissible actions; in the field of ethics there also exists pluralism of various perceptions. We often disagree on whether a specific action should be regarded as a morally-admissible act or not. This is not surprising since there exist various convictions and beliefs about life and the world. Despite all this we should be aware of the fact that we co-exist and shape our society together, so we have to agree which common values our society will strive for. This ethic minimum or world ethos is one of the preconditions for mutual dialogue. At this point one should enumerate a few basic principles which are founded on the respect for human dignity and which, also, advocate the untouchability of human life –these include the following:

1. All human lives are equally important and they should be treated as such.
2. One should never kill an unborn child.
3. Human life should be perceived as a precious gift.

Key words: anthropology, ethics, compassion, dignity of a person, world ethos, philosophy of religion.

Mark Kleyman

AM I CHARLIE? RELIGION, TRUTH AND TOLERANCE IN MULTICULTURAL URBAN NEIGHBOURHOODS

Abstract: The current situation in Europe is characterized by the diasporization of urban neighborhoods. As a consequence, the distant stranger is increasingly becoming a next-door neighbor, who shares the street, public facilities, workplace and school. At the same time, the series of terrorist attacks and refugee crisis produce the widespread disbelief in democracy as the best road to the solution of the most haunting social problems. This inevitably emphasizes the need of rethinking the very essence of democracy. The paper puts an emphasis on the need of cultivating the idea of solidary personalism, which, in many respects, is rooted back to Albert Schweitzer's appeal for the Reverence for Life and Leo Tolstoy's reliance upon non-resistance to evil by force. Solidary personalism may be regarded as a basic ethical principle of emerging grassroots democracy within multicultural urban neighborhoods.

Key words: diasporization; urban neighborhood; multiculturalism; solidary personalism; tolerance.

Vojko Strahovnik

TRUTH, HISTORY, INTEGRITY, AND RECONCILIATION

Abstract: The article explores the relationship between historical truth, integrity, and reconciliation. As regards the concept of truth, it focuses on the narrative conditionality of historical truth. Next, the importance of truth and truthfulness for integrity of community is highlighted. Destruction or falsification of the history of a particular group of people is a type of crime against them; such lies could and often do undermine the integrity of the national or other community. The respect for historical truth is thus a prerequisite for reconciliation processes at the community level.

Key words: truth, historical truth, narrative, integrity, reconciliation.

Jože Dežman

LIVING IN A LIE

Abstract: In Titoism – Second Yugoslavia (1945-1990) – the society was split into the new, governing communist class and the segregated, discriminated and stigmatised social groups that the authorities defined using different measures. The basic differentiation between the privileged by the regime and the ones marginalized was introduced via various taboos. Out of nearly 100.000 casualties of the War, civil war and the revolutionary terror between 1941 and 1946, more than 40,000 of the dead were tabooed: more than 25,000 of those were murdered by the partisans during the War and after it or were other victims of the civil war, and more than 15,000 Slovenians died while mobilized in the occupators' armies, victims of allied air strikes etc. The relatives of these victims were punished collectively, unable to freely develop and impeded in day to day life. The political police maintained this racist division of the population into those privileged by the system and those seen as worthless all the way until the dissolution of Titoism. Even today, the figureheads of the regime, particularly the leaders of the Communist Party/League of Communists and political police lie that they "did not know" about the mass and individual murders between and after the War. However the taboo was never capable of concealing the crimes of Titoism. As an example: I have analysed over 1500 cases from the Archives of the Commission for the implementation of Redressing of Injustices Act, of how the tabooed victims were declared dead in courts between 1945 and 1990, with more than 1690 people declared dead, as they would declare up to 5 murdered people at once. The analysis of the proceedings shows that the regime's lie "we didn't know" could never stand. However, the relatives of the murdered victims had to lie in these court proceedings, having to hide from the government what they actually knew about the fates of their loved ones. Thousands of judges and policemen who knew the truth were also forced to lie. They all knew the truth, and had to lie. This was a part of living in a lie in Titoism.

Key words: Slovenia, Titoism, tabooed victims 1941-1946, dissolution of Titoism's taboos, transitional justice.

Béla Mester

SYMPATHY WITH OTHER'S PRIDE - AN ADDITION FOR THE POLITICS OF RECOGNITION

Abstract: A characteristic feature of the classical model of *toleration*, rooted in the ideas of the political philosophy of the early modernity is a privileged epistemological position of the person who formulates the ideas and rules of the tolerant behaviour, and opinions. It is inevitable that it emerges as a point of view of an *omniscient spectator* whose position is above all the interests, *pride*s, faiths, superstitions and customs of the people as the subjects of this system of toleration. In the previous writing of mine within the framework of the same series of books, I have analysed the structure of the key text of this discourse, Locke's *A Letter Concerning Toleration* from the point of view of the position of the author as a *spectator*. In several former writings of mine, I have analysed several features of the classical religious *toleration* from the point of view of the *pictorial philosophy*. In a recent paper, I have analysed the historical narrative of the *religio duplex* formulated by Jan Assmann, in his recent monograph. All of my investigations have finished in the same result about the structure of the classical model of toleration; within the framework of this concept we can tolerate things and phenomena which are meaningless and valueless for ourselves, regardless to the value and meaning which appears for the people whose behaviour and opinions we tolerate. This kind of *toleration* must neglect the *pride* and *identity* of the people who are tolerated by us. In my lecture I will analyse the possibilities of a new concept of *toleration* within the frame of *politics of recognition*, connected with the points of view of the values and elements of *identity* of the culture of the tolerated people. A thing for toleration for us can be a thing for *pride* for other people

Key words: identity, pictorial philosophy, politics of recognition, pride, religio duplex, uninterested spectator, toleration.

Gábor Kovács

'IT IS POSSIBLE TO ATTAIN TRUTH THROUGH A WAY PAVED BY LIES' – THE HISTORICAL TRAJECTORY OF COMMUNISM FROM COMPASSION AND TRUTH-SEEKING TO THE TOTALITARIAN TERROR

Abstract: What was communism: a pseudo-religion promising this-worldly salvation, an ideology of modernization promising a quick catching up for backward regions, or a terroristic regime killing millions of innocent victims? These are the aspects of an historical phenomenon, the emergence of which induced an array of explanative schemes. Ernest Gellner gives a sociological explanation focusing on the special historical-social and political situation of Central and Eastern Europe. Hannah Arendt produces a philosophical explication. She raises the question: How was it possible that Marxian emancipatory philosophy, the heir of the Enlightenmen,t begot a terroristic totalitarian political system as the Stalinist socialism? According to her explanation, impersonal pity, which was one of the main motives of Jacobine revolutionaries, the predecessors of Bolsheviks, involved the contempt of real individual human life, and led to the sacrifice of it for the sake of abstract, inhuman ideals. What is most interesting is the psychological structure of the communist believer for whom this ideology was a pseudo religious creed requiring from him/her a total intellectual-moral conversion. It was true in the case of a very acute minded man, as Georg Lukács, a Hungarian philosopher, was, who during some months went through the process of this overall conversion. There is impossible to accept Bolshevism, he wrote in 1918 citing Dostoyevsky's hero from *Crime and Punishment*, because it tries to attain truth through a way paved by lies. In a short time, as already a believer of new revolutionary ideology, he cited Judith, the heroine of Hebbel's drama who says before killing of Holofernes: "When God has put the sin between me and my action, how would I dare to abstain myself from it'. It is a terrible idea but illustrates well the strange intertwining of fatalism, moral conviction, and inhuman cruelty so characteristic for the communist intellectuals of the time.

Key words: compassion, truth, lie, communism, conversion.

Simon Malmenvall

GEORGES FLOROVSKY AND RUSSIAN INTELLECTUAL HISTORY: REJECTION OF ORTHODOXY AS A WAY TOWARDS THE BOLSHEVIK REVOLUTION?

Abstract: This article aims at presenting the historiographical-philosophical views of Georges Florovsky (1893–1979), Russian theologian, philosopher and historian. His views originate in the normativity of patristic theology and argue that from the 16th century onwards the Russian thought was "in captivity" imposed by the Western influences. Among the foreign influences the 19th-century idealist philosophy is seen by Florovsky as the one having gravest effects: its loss of historical consciousness paved the way for various utopistic projects, including the Bolshevik revolution in 1917. These "dead ends" supposedly originate in the false ecclesiology of the intellectual leaders of the Orthodox Church who tended to separate theology and philosophy from the sacramental-liturgical life. The author of this article accepts the views of Florovsky as reasonable, yet at the same time partial. This is due to the fact that his views are concerned with the intellectual environment which favoured the rise of Bolshevism on the Russian soil, without taking into consideration the complexity of the Russian society at the turn of 19-20th century.

Key words: Georges Florovsky, Ways of Russian Theology, Orthodox Church, history of Russia, Bolshevism, revolution.

Mateja Pevec Rozman

TRUTH AND COMPASSION ON THE HORIZON OF INTERPERSONAL RELATIONSHIPS AND PERSONAL RESPONSIBILITY

Abstract: The "classical" scholastic definition of truth is *veritas est adaequatio intellectus et rei,* truth is the equation of intellect and thing. The ontological truth of being, however, is the possibility to think about being. This notion of truth allows us to talk about truth that *belongs* to being. Truth is being given to us primarily in our experience of interpersonallity, that is, in our relationship with the O(o)ther. Interpersonal relations show themselves on the horizon where truth is unfolded. From this ontological perspective compassion could be seen as being compassionate, or even to suffer with another being when a lack of being or an ontological privation (absence) is present. This paper attempts to reexamine the postmodern understanding of truth, that argues that truth cannot be expressed, nor reached, and thinks of truth as being beyond our own being. But if human being is thrown into existence, compassion reveals itself in the limitations of beings, that we face, as a possibility to understand the existentials of fear and terror. Being is therefore being(-there) with others. It demands a compassionate relationship. The precondition of compassion is accepting the truth about the other - an act that is possible only through an openness for a relation(ship) with the other. Such a relationship must be an ethical relationship, otherwise compassion is not possible. Compassion extends into responsibility, which is essentially active and not passive. The main focus of this paper is a new approach towards the understanding of truth and compassion. The paper follows Emmanuel Levinas' understanding of the other and the relationship with the other, detailed in his work *Time and the Other.* The author aims to invert the understanding of the truth – compassion binomial and proposes understanding of truth as something that is being given to us in the face-to-face encounter with the other.

Key words: truth, compassion, other, responsibility, relationship, the feminine.

Erika Prijatelj
COMPASSION AS A WAY OF LIVING THE TRUTH

Abstract: This paper presents the existence of a strong interconnectedness between truth and compassion, demonstrating the static and dynamic dimensions of both. It moves beyond the limits of dualistic thinking and offers compassion as a way to seek truth through daily practice. By doing so, compassion can now be seen as a qualitatively new approach toward discovering truth. The paper posits that compassion needs to be demonstrated at the individual as well as at the collective level. The intensity and depth of the societal compassion is the barometer of the moral healthiness of any community, society or nation.

Key words: compassion, truth, static, dynamic, justice, suffering, happiness.

Marcin Godawa
CHRISTIAN-SPIRITUAL WAY OUT OF ANTHROPOLOGICAL COMPASSION TRAP

Abstract: Against all the positive aspects of the question of compassion [empathy, tolerance] it can also arise the anthropological compassion trap when one's understanding and help are confined only to human capacities while the divine grace is the effective and gentle way-out. Walking the way of grace leaves the horizon of half-truth or illusion so as to attain the gift of full-truth about man confirmed by a form of spiritual healing in accordance with the theological order. The aim of my presentation is to expose the liberating role of grace in two dimensions. Firstly, in accordance with Christian theology I am going to present the concept of grace along with some particular questions of its cooperation with man's efforts in the context of leaving the compassion trap. Secondly, I would like to illustrate the problem by the analysis of St. Augustine's clear example.

Key words: compassion, truth, divine grace, effective and gentle agent, peace of heart.

Tomaž Erzar and Katarina Kompan Erzar
THE PROCESS OF FORGIVENESS: "NO MORE A SERVANT, BUT A SON"

Abstract: In the paper different views on forgiveness and tensions inherent in practicing forgiveness are discussed. Traditionally, forgiveness is linked with reconciling with offenders and fulfilling one's moral duty. Psychologists, however, consider forgiveness to be an intrapsychic endeavor helping victims to let go of negative feelings and grudges. Using three parables from the New Testament, the authors argue that opposing views on forgiveness represent different aspects of a single process in which persons who have been wronged abandon the position of helpless victims and assume the position of moral agents. Also presented is the idea that the duty of Christian forgiveness applies to those who no more perceive themselves as servants, but as sons of the Father and brothers.

Key words: forgiveness, reconciliation, New Testament, victimhood, parables.

Roman Globokar
TRUTH AND COMPASSION WHEN REVERSING A LIFE DECISION

Abstract: There comes a certain point when an individual defines their future life with a free and conscious life decision. In moral theology, a life decision is mostly defined as a decision to pursue either a married or consecrated life and is also marked by a public ceremony. It should be a unique decision that permanently commits an individual or a married couple to be faithful to their decision. However, it is a fact that an increasing number of young people do not make such final decisions anymore; additionally, more and more people are reversing their life decisions. How can the Church community and the moral theologians belonging to it respond to such challenges? The participants in the Synod of Bishops on the Family in Rome in October 2015 faced a dilemma regarding the question of including the divorced and remarried, and whether to stress the truth of Church doctrine or stress showing mercy to individual people. A pastoral solution must originate from a solid basis of Church doctrine. It is to answer these questions that the elaboration on the topic of "life decisions" made by moral theologian Klaus Demmer (1931–2014) will be presented. A possible solution for the divorced and remarried is dispensation that applies to priests and members of religious communities and with which the Church authority, after a certain amount of time and careful consideration, enables former priests and members of religious communities to marry in the Church. The analysis of the Final Report of the Synod follows with the indication of possible solutions suggested by the participants.

Key words: life decision, truth, marriage, indissolubility, dispensation, synod on the family, mercy.

Stanislav Slatinek
MISUSE OF TRUTH IN THE MARRIAGE AND ITS FATAL CONSEQUENCES

Abstract: The aim of the discussion is to draw attention to the abuse of truth in the marriage and its fatal consequences, according to the judgments of the Court of the Roman Rota (1993–2003). The truth in the marriage is being abused when one fiancé makes deceitful efforts to mislead another fiancé into marriage. The purpose of the deceitful fiancé, is to obtain a certain benefit, i.e. the marriage. Due to the false illusions about himself, deceitful fiancé seriously harms another fiancé, the children and the marriage itself, that can never become a loving marriage relationship. The discussion shows different types of scams and consequences that mostly affect the children who are born in such a marriage.

Key words: deceitful fraud, void marriage, abuse of truth, the Roman Rota, fiancé.

AUTHORS

Jože Dežman, PhD, Upper Carniola Museum, Kranj, Slovenia.

Tomaž Erzar, PhD, Associate Professor, Faculty of Theology, University of Ljubljana, Slovenia.

Katarina Kompan Erzar, PhD, Assistant Professor, Faculty of Theology, University of Ljubljana, Slovenia.

Stanko Gerjolj, Full Professor, University of Ljubljana, Faculty of Theology, Slovenia.

Roman Globokar, Assistant Professor, Faculty of Theology, University of Ljubljana, Slovenia.

Marcin Godawa, Dr Hab., Associate Professor, The Pontifical University of John Paul II in Krakow, Poland.

Anton Jamnik, Associate Professor, University of Ljubljana, Faculty of Theology, Slovenia.

Mark Kleyman, PhD (Candidate of Sciences) in Social Psychology, Associate Professor (Docent), Department of Philosophy, Ivanovo State University of Chemistry and Technology, Russia.

Gábor Kovács, Senior Research Fellow; Institute of Philosophy; Research Centre for the Humanities; Hungarian Academy of Sciences, Hungary.

Marcel V. Măcelaru, Prof. Dr., Founding President, Institute for Faith and Human Flourishing, Timişoara, Romania and Professor of Old Testament, Institutul Teologic Penticostal, Bucharest, Romania.

Simon Malmenvall, BA in Russian studies and history, MA in social and cultural history (Faculty of Arts, University of Ljubljana), Doctoral student of theology (Faculty of Theology, University of Ljubljana), Slovenia.

Béla Mester, Ph.D., Senior Research Fellow of the Institute of Philosophy, Research Centre for the Humanities, Hungarian Academy of Sciences, Budapest, Hungary; share-time associate professor of the University of

Nyíregyháza, Hungary; vice-president of the Hungarian Philosophical Society, Hungary.

Robert Petkovšek, Associate Professor, University of Ljubljana, Faculty of Theology, Slovenia.

Mateja Pevec Rozman, Assistant Professor, University of Ljubljana (Faculty of Theology), Slovenia.

Erika Prijatelj, Assistant Professor, University of Ljubljana (Faculty of Theology), Slovenia.

Stanislav Slatinek, Assistant Professor, University of Ljubljana (Faculty of Theology), Slovenia.

Vojko Strahovnik, Assistant Professor and Research Associate University of Ljubljana, Faculty of Theology, Slovenia.

Bojan Žalec, Research Professor of Philosophy, Faculty of Theology, University of Ljubljana, Slovenia.

REVIEWS

The book *Truth and Compassion* edited by Robert Petkovšek and Bojan Žalec is an excellent book offering lucid, comprehensive, and engaging discussion of the topics related to truth and compassion. The book includes perspectives of theology, philosophy, history, psychology, and law in a way that it often entangles them and stimulates a dialogue among them, which is also a precondition for dealing with such a complex topic. The starting point of the book is a creed that truth and compassion are intimately connected in a way that on the one hand compassion helps us to reach some of the important aspect of truth, and on the other that lies and related phenomena often hinder our compassioned stance both on the personal level as well as on the level of the society as a whole (flourishment and integrity of the community). Several essays convincingly argue in this general direction, employing diverse theoretical perspectives and focusing on specific historical and societal experiences. Other supplement such a direction by focusing on origins of violence, forgiveness, and reconciliation. To conclude I assert that the present book is an important, innovative, and original scientific contribution in the field and can only recommend engaging with it.

Michal Valčo, Associate Professor of Religious Studies, Faculty of Humanities, University of Žilina, Slovakia

Monografija je na vrhunski zanstveni ravni. Njeni avtorji opozarjajo na povezanost resnice in sočutja ter dokazujejo tako pogubnost njune odsotnosti ali zlorabe po eni strani kot tudi zdravilnost in odrešilnost njunega gojenja na drugi strani. Resnico in sočutje, ter njuno vzajemno prepletenost, raziskujejo z različnih vidikov: filozofskega, teološkega, religiološkega, zgodovinskega in idejno-zgodovinskega, psihoterapevtskega, edukacijskega in pravnega. Dobro je predstavljena raznolikost obeh glavnih predmetov: njune vrste in oblike, ravni, raznoteri dejavniki, funkcije ter tudi pomen, ki sta ga imela v zgodovini. Prispevke odlikuje visoka znanstvena metodološka raven, vključno s poznavanjem relevantne znanstvene literature in z ustreznim tehničnim aparatom navajanja. Knjiga prinaša mnoga znanstveno preverjena oz. utemeljena spoznanja in rešitve. Izrazoslovje je zelo raznoliko in bogato. Bralec na enem mestu dobi večplastno analizo, interpretacijo, primerjavo in aplikacijo široke množice terminov oz. pojmov. Obstaja malo del o pojavih, obravnavanih v tej knjigi, ki lahko bralca tako terminološko oz. pojmovno obogatijo.

Tema monografije je izredno pomemebna tako z vidika slovenske pretekle in sedanje situacije kot tudi z aspekta evropskega in globalnega položaja. Resnica in sočutje sta ključna pojma našega premisleka o slovenski preteklosti in urejanja njenih posledic v sedanjosti. Enako velja za urejanje najbolj perečih evropskih in globalnih problemov, npr. begunske oz. migrantske krize. Problemi, ki so povezani z resnico in sočutjem (ti pojavi so med seboj tesno prepleteni, kar je razvidno tudi iz zadevne monografije), so zelo težki in njihova nerazrešenost še kako pesti sodobnost. Vsi ti pojavi so zelo kompleksni in skrivajo v sebi številne pasti, zato jih je potrebno čim bolj natančno in celostno spoznavati in razumeti, da bomo lahko ustrezno ravnali in ukrepali. Zadevna knjiga bo zaradi svoje znanstvene verodostojnosti in novih spoznanj, ki jih prinaša, nedvomno v veliko pomoč ne samo ožjemu krogu strokovnjakov, ampak tudi drugim, ki se tako ali drugače srečujejo s problemi, povezanimi z glavnimi temami monografije. V slovenski zgodovini in sedanjosti sta resnica in sočutje, ter njuni odnosi, igrali oz. igrata izredno pomembno vlogo, tudi z vidika nasilja, sprave in miru. To je dobro razvidno iz evidence, ki jo prinaša knjiga. V znanstvenem prostoru primanjkuje del, ki te teme obravnavajo po eni strani tako celostno, interdisciplinarno in v medsebojni povezanosti, po drugi strani pa hkrati na tako visoki znanstveni ravni. Knjiga je posebna zaradi svoje kompleksne, večplastne in tudi podrobne, pa vendarle celostne obravnave. Vendar pa brez takega integralnega pristopa tematike knjige ni mogoče primerno razumeti.

Ugotavljam, da gre za zelo kakovostno znanstveno delo, ki so ga napisali znanstveniki, od katerih so mnogi že dobro uveljavljeni tudi na evropski ravni. Odlikuje jo strnjenost in jasnost prispevkov. Kljub kompleksnosti tematike in predmetov obravnave avtorjem uspe svoje argumente in dognanja podati na razmeroma nezapleten način, kolikor je na vrhunski znanstveni ravni to seveda mogoče. Monografiji pripada visoka ocena z vidika znanstvene verodostojnosti, aktualnosti in novih spoznanj, ki jih prinaša, prispevala pa bo tudi k uveljavitvi in ugledu slovenske znanosti v tujini. Zato menim, da si zasluži finančno podporo s strani ARRS, in le-to zelo priporočam.

Ciril Sorč, Retired Full Professor of Dogmatic Theology, Faculty of Theology, University of Ljubljana, Slovenia